Giggles

To order additional copies, please contact us.
BookSurge, LLC
www.booksurge.com
1-866-308-6235
orders@booksurge.com

Giggles

A NOVEL

Mimi Brown

2005

Giggles

In dedication to, Frank my husband of thirty-two years and my best friend in life; and our greatest gifts, who are precious and loving daughters, Amy and Angela. My son-in-law, Don who is a wonderful husband and father. To my grandchildren Kalyn and Kaleb, who give me so much joy and pleasure in my life. Most of all, I thank God for this family, a gift I will always cherish and never take for granted. To my parents, Loren and Alice and Frank's parents, Bill (deceased 1993) and Gladys, also family members, I want to express deepest thanks and appreciation for all your love, understanding, support, and help that you gave and continue on giving. To my sister Sandi, thank you, for our sisterly time together and your inspiration. To my brother Loren, thank you for reading my first draft and words of encouragement.

And also to our good friends: Sue and Ken and to our childhood friends, Jodie and John

"True friends are like diamonds precious but rare."
False friends are like autumn leaves found everywhere."
Author unknown

The above quotation was on a plaque that was given to us by Rich, Frank's childhood friend and our dearest friend and confidant, who passed away on December 18,1991. We truly miss you.

PRELUDE

The carpet was old and faded, once being the colors of tangerine and gilt. Design patterns, unrecognizable, with the centered seam that divided the small dining room from a rather larger living room, where many footsteps had once walked, before the new tenants. Walls once painted a brilliant gold now looked dim from long years of past scrubbing. Several pairs of second-hand orange flowered curtains hung adequately at windows that were previously once used as an enclosed porch. The larger room was filled with pieces of furniture such as a two tone brown recliner with matching ottoman, along with a small wooden and marble coffee table and a three foot wooden lamp that were purchased from the classified ads in a local newspaper. Other obtained pieces were two round lamp tables, a reddish-orange rocking chair and a turquoise sectional sofa, bought from deceased grandparents. All the above had created a mix matched decorum.

Kneeling on the thinned worn out carpeting, the young woman leaned against the side of one of the two chairs and glanced up at the painting on the wall beside him. There hung tawdry colored oil depicting an old black man fishing from a riverbank that was scattered with trash. For the young woman the picture was not a favorite. Still this one picture was appreciated by both and because it was a wedding gift. This was the only wall ornament that hung in their sparsely decorated living room.

Slowly turning her attention back to the young man sitting comfortably in his recliner with his legs stretched out upon the haggard and faded footstool. For a few seconds the couple's eyes locked and neither one of them spoken a word.

Taking a deep breath, she placed her hands on the arm of his chair, feeling with her fingertips the silken raised threads. He turned away and reached for another cigarette. The only sounds that the woman became aware of were the noises of the lid of his cigarette lighter clicking shut and the shifting movements he made in his chair.

Her knees were aching from the unpadded carpeting, so she lowered herself to the floor. Waiting patiently for his response, she looked down at her restless hands. When only silenced lingered, his young wife slowly raised her head and saw that the husband's eyes were still closed; looking as if he might had fallen asleep. Realizing a few seconds later, that he was just deep in thought, pondering over the question while holding his cigarette.

"What can he be thinking about? Could he possibly be reflecting on that it's just too soon for another baby? Or perhaps maybe because we're both yet still young?" she thought." But I want this second child now! I don't feel or think that it's too soon." She said to herself. "Our children would be close to three years apart. Oh God, you know in my heart, this is what I want! But the question is, does he? Does my husband really want another child at this time? He's only twenty."

Her thoughts were finally interrupted by the way he would put his cigarette out against the side of the ashtray. She just couldn't wait any longer for him to be the first to break the silence and start talking. To be more comfortable, the woman got up from her sitting position on the floor and sat down next to his outstretched legs on the ottoman to face him.

Looking directly into his eyes she asked, "What do you think Frank?" The young husband's response to his wife was, "Dianna, I think we should perhaps try to discuss this more thoroughly." He had thought hopefully that he had chosen his words carefully, while she sat and watched him roll another cigarette against the inside of the ashtray. Leaning forward a little she reached out and gently touched his arm. Giving him a nervous smile she asked, "If possible wouldn't you want to have a son? Besides you said that you and your cousin are the only ones to carry on the family name."

***

"That's right, but that's not the important issue here." He said.

***

Looking anxious and intently at him she said, "All right, I know, but..."

MORE KISSES

"Oh Angie", she helplessly signed. "Time to go, you help mom, simultaneously signing with her hands and talking to her twelve year old daughter, while trying to pack the clothes and other personal belongings into suitcases, bags and boxes that laid open and tossed upon the bed. Ignoring her mother, Angie grabbed another item of hers out from one of the suitcases and angrily stuffed it back into the empty dresser drawer. In her disturbed state of confusion, she begins to stomp from bed to dresser, whining and hitting herself in the face and chest, while biting at her hands leaving very bad red marks.

Angie's mother noticed her distress and stopped abruptly from the packing and slowly walked over to the other side of the room to stand near her daughter. Trying to keep calm and holding back from her own tears, Angie's mom reached out to put her hand gently on her daughter's shoulder to reassure her by giving a rub or massage that everything would be all right. Sometimes mom knew there were moments that a gentle touch could calm Angie down. But at this moment mom's tenderness with her hand had only caused a negative reaction from her daughter. For Angie had pulled herself away with a quick jerk of her arm and started biting at her hands while she vocalized. Mom stepped back some and walked over to the bed to continue with the unfinished packing. She allowed herself while working to repeat the needed skills of signing, using face expressions along with body language or movements in order for her daughter to understand that it was necessary for them to finish what they were doing. Since early that morning Angie was told about going in the truck, with dad, mom and sister, taking her belongings, to meet some new friends to help her; and that these new friends would help all of them to make Angie happy. Although it was very hard for mom to relate this information for the pain was deep within her soul. She knew with her daughter leaving their home for the needed help and care just made the ache only deeper. Once again mom moved away from the bed and slowly advanced towards her daughter. But not to her surprise in seeing how her little girl pulled away whimpering like a trapped animal and still continuing with the self- abuse.

Angie had dropped to her knees on the floor expressing her emotions very loud while biting at her hands and arms, while hitting at her face and chest. She grabbed and pulled at her hair as well. Her mother signed, "stop please" as Angie looked up. For the twisted up look on her face related the feelings of anger, confusion and pain. Slowly mom knelt down in front of her daughter and signed, "I love you." Angie looked at her mother while still biting at her hands. Again mom signed, "love you" and "no bite hurt hand." She moved her own hand slowly up towards her daughter's face and gently touched her cheek. After a brief moment feeling tired and stiff mom stood back up and walked over to the bedroom window. She glanced up at the sky and started whispering to share her inner thoughts.

I know Angie you want your things left in your own room. It should be that way, if only you were. Feeling so heart broken and defeated she said louder.

***

"God, she just doesn't understand what's happening here. How could she? There's really no way for me to explain to her that she's going to live somewhere else. I feel so helpless. I don't want Angie to feel that her family abandoning her. Please God, please."

***

She turned from the window and saw that her daughter was beginning to calm down and unwillingly walked back to the bed. She glanced down at her daughter's possession in cases and boxes.

"I can't do this! I don't want to do this!" She sobbed. With eyes blurred she forced herself to continue with the task of packing. She felt the pain so deep in her heart, the same pain she knew that her daughter would feel later. She tried so desperately not to show her grief through her actions or to wear those emotions upon her face. It was very hard but she soon pulled herself together and said, "God, please help me now to help my family to get through this evening. Please, help me dear Lord believe that what I'm doing will be the best thing for my little girl. Someday please let my daughter be truly happy."

A little while later Angie had ceased her attempts to unpack her things and for a few moments stood calmly observing her mother. The thought that perhaps her daughter's fit of rage had finally ended and maybe she had accepted. Mom looked quickly around the bedroom to make sure she didn't forget any of the special treasures, especially the clown collection. Only a few of the most favorite ones would accompany her.

But as mom started to pick up the things upon the bed, her daughter

4

abruptly slammed the palms of her hands upon the dresser. She paused momentarily to stare at her reflection in the dresser mirror. Mom too looked at the face that is distorted with much anger; confusion and the wild tear filled eyes. The stares were broken even though Angie continued the self-abuse to her hands.

The young woman walked over and stood beside her daughter and signed, "hands and hurt." Angie stopped and giggled. Mom had tenderly had given her little girl a kiss on the cheek. Angie responded by giggling and she proceeded to place her arm around mom's neck and pulled her mother toward her for a kiss. The mother held her so tight because she knew that soon she would have to let her daughter go.

"I love you so much, Angie. I'm here no matter what. If only when I let go, I could wake up and all of this would be a bad dream. And you would be my normal, twelve your old daughter." Said mom.

She fought back the tears as she released her and signed, "I love you." Angie returned the sign for "love" and giggled once more. Her mother turned and quickly walked over to the bed for one more final examination of boxes, bags and cases.

Than without looking back, she walked out of her daughter's bedroom and into the hallway. Near the stairway she called for her husband. "Frank, can you come and get Angie's bags now?" Silently she whispered to herself. "God, please, let me get through this! Help us all!" Then a second time she called for Angie's dad. "Frank! Hurry up please, I don't want for her to become upset again."

A disturbing noise behind made her turn around from the stairway and saw Angie coming out of the bedroom on her knees, whimpering and slapping herself in the chest with one hand while biting at the other. Once again mom took notice of the situation and signed to her. "Please, stand up!" Moving slowly toward Angie she soothingly patted her on the back and signed, "Dad, get bags, put in truck. Yes?" Although the signed words still made Angie looked at her mother with a rather confused gesture and signed, "Yes."

Frank came to the top of the stairs and saw his wife and daughter standing together in the hallway. He walked into the room looking straight at the bed. There he saw all the suitcases, bags and boxes that were scattered upon the spread. He raised his voice a little and asked his wife, "Dianna, is this everything?" "Yes," she answered over her shoulder. She turned back to maneuver her daughter towards the stairway. In a rush voice mom said to dad as the two of them stopped on the top landing.

"Frank, go ahead and take her things down stairs. It's all right to start and warm the truck. While you are doing that, I will get the coats and others things from the closet."

Angie stood on the top landing and looked into the long mirror that hung perpendicular on the wall. She watched her mother stepped aside from her and descended down the stairs to the bottom landing to open the closet door. She continued to watch and observe while mom reached in and pulled out a winter coat along with her own coat. Angie made a vocal sound to get some attention and then quickly turned away from the mirror and started attacking at her hands again.

Dianna closed the closet door and turned and looked up at her daughter. She smiled up at Angie, but did not sign for her to come down stairs. For she knew that in her daughter's own time she would follow because the actions already told mom not to rush her little girl. Instead Dianna forced herself to turn and walked down the remaining step to the living room. She saw Frank's dad, Papa sitting quietly in the rocker. He did not looked up and he seemed oblivious to the commotion that went on upstairs. He glanced up in the direction of his daughter-in-law and she noticed the sad, helpless expression on his face. To break the awkward silence within the room Dianna says aloud, "Well Papa, I think that we are almost ready to go soon. Angie should be on her way down after she's finished looking at herself in the mirror. She did have a very hard time dealing with the packing. I think and hope that she might begin to calm down," as she continued with her rattling on, while trying extremely hard not to show her emotions and tears. "Ah dad, I'm not sure how long we will be gone."

✱✱✱

"That's all right, you and Frank take your time and do what is necessary." Said Papa.

✱✱✱

'Would you and mom please have some coffee with us when we get back?"

✱✱✱

"Sure thing," responded Papa. "Don't worry about anything. We'll take care of things here."

***

"And dad, could you make sure Duke gets outside while we're gone?" Papa's daughter-in-law concerned about the family dog.

***

"Sure thing, I can do that for you, don't worry," says Papa.

***

Hearing the familiar chime and ticking sound coming from the mantel clock, a treasured gift given from Frank's dad to the family, Dianna immediately turned around to check on the time. She said to herself. "It's 11:00 A.M. Angie has to be there by late afternoon. Oh God, time is going too fast! Please help us especially Angie. Hear my prayer."

"What can I help you with Di?" Asked Frank's mom, Nana, coming through the dining room from the kitchen, with the dog following close at her heels. She just wants to be so helpful when there's nothing anyone can really do. But where would this young couple be all those early years without the love and support from their parents?

"No. Not a thing mom, just you and Papa could be here for us when we get back. I told dad wasn't sure on what time though."

Picking up one of the coats from the couch, Dianna remembered and returned to the bottom landing and called up the stairway to her oldest daughter. "Amy, are you ready? It's time for us to leave!" Amy had been in her bedroom most of the morning getting ready physically and emotionally.

***

"Just a second mom," she yelled back.

***

At the top of the stairs Angie stood. She was admiring herself in the landing mirror and perhaps waiting for her sister. For the time being she had forgotten her trauma. She stood before the mirror and giggled, while fussing with her hair and opened her mouth wide to utter some vocal sounds.

Amy walked out of her bedroom down the hallway to the top landing, paused momentarily behind her sister and regarded the actions in the mirror. Angie turned toward her sister and patted her own hair then signed "nice." Amy repeated the sign, "nice", as she gives her little sister a hug.

At the bottom of the stairs mom clutched at Angie's blue winter coat and watched her two lovely and spirited daughters at the top of the stairway. She thought that they needed a few moments together and hesitated to hurry them up. The girls' mother wanted this time for them to be special, remembered and imprinted in their hearts.

Amy being the big sister she was helped to fix and smoothed her sister's hair. She took a small step back and signed to Angie. "Hair pretty." She smiled, signed and said out loud, " let me fix the collar of your sweater. Oh your pants are twisted too." Amy attempted to straighten out sister's clothes with difficulty because of Angie's wiggles and giggles. She gave her sister a frustrated look and signed, "Wait, help you fix pants." Angie responded by tipping back her head and puckered her lips for a kiss. Their mother watched from the bottom of the landing with tears in her eyes. She continued to observe her two daughters while she wished that moment would last forever.

***

"Di, are you and the girls ready?" Asked Frank, as he joined his wife on the stairway landing and placed a loving arm around her shoulders.

***

"Oh, Frank." Said his wife, a little startled. "I didn't hear you come in. Do you have the truck warmed?"

***

"Yes. Is there anything else of Angie's that needs to go out in the truck?"

***

She turned just slightly to look at her husband and said, "Everything off the bed upstairs, you didn't leave anything behind?"

***

"I didn't leave a thing," he said, still with his protective arm around his wife.

***

"How about her portable television. I had it sitting on the kitchen table?"

***

"It's already in the truck bed," said Frank. Quietly, he stood there holding his wife while they both watched their daughters.

***

"Mom, how's this look?" asked Amy from the top of the stairs, where she had been making the final touches on her sister.

***

"Looks nice Amy," mom answered while Frank removed his arm from his wife's shoulder and signed "nice and pretty" to Angie. "Amy, can you help your sister down? We have to leave now."

Amy turned toward Angie and signed, "come, time to go." She then motioned to Angie to go before her and the two girls started down the stairway.

Quietly the girls' mother whispered to their dad once again, "Frank, are we doing the right thing? I'm scared."

***

"I really don't know. I hope we are. I'm scared too. But we got to remember it's what's best's for Angie. We'll get through this together. All of us."

As the two sisters descended from the stairs, Angie became upset once more. She started to make loud vocal noises and she bit at her left hand while she pounded the stairway wall with her other hand. When Angie finally reached the last step she sat down and slapped at her chest. Amy joined her sister on the bottom step and put a consoling arm around her little sister's shoulder. She then signed to Angie "O.K., love you."

The parents knew of their oldest daughter's ability to calm her sister's moods. So together they left the living room and joined Nana with Papa in the kitchen. Frank who seemed and looked defeated sat down at the table while his father walked slowly over to the back door. Papa too looked defeated for not being able to help his son at that particular time. He stood at the door staring out the window with his hands in his pockets jiggling his change. Papa could hear his wife speaking comforting words to their son and his young wife.

Dianna stood in the middle of the kitchen shaking with uncontrollable tears with her hands hiding the face of grief, twelve years of pain and emotional stress along with the many scars of turmoil while battling the fight to keep her little girl at home. When she heard her husband's words, " Di, please pull your self together, stop crying now." She wiped at the last tears for the time being, later she knew the time would be right to empty out those painful feelings. There was a slight and tender pat upon her back from his mother. That touch made her glance over at her husband and at his mom. She than looked into at the eyes of a good and loving woman, who had been there for them so many times.

"Di, everything will be alright," said Nana, standing close by and putting an arm around her son's wife. The younger woman's lips quivered while she returned a hug saying, "I know mom. It's just so very hard."

From Duke's laying position in front of the wood burner in the dining room he sensed the emotional atmosphere and got up and trotted over to Frank. His tail wagged rapidly and he placed his short, stubby front paws on Frank's knee. Duke cocked his head up at his master to catch his attention. He was a comical sight with one ear bent back and the other ear hung down. Frank reached forward and scratched behind the dog's ears. Duke loved the attention from Frank while moving even closer. Temporarily they allowed their lives to be mused upon that moment.

Then, the tranquility was broken by Angie's sounds of frustration. Hard to describe and very changeable, her voice goes from a resonant barely audible low sounding tone of uh; progressing to a higher pitch frequency tone of ah; sometimes transforming into a dull, brokenhearted whimper. Her varying moods are translated by these different vocal tones.

***

"Mom!" Angie won't stand up," yelled Amy.

***

"O.K. honey. We'll be right in there, go put on your coat. Dad and I will help your sister."

Frank stood up and left the kitchen and walked into the living room. He approached Angie slowly so not to upset her further. Looking down at his daughter he signed " Stand up!" She ignored him and bit at her hands. Her father remained firm and signed once more to his daughter, "Stand up! Time put coat on." For a few seconds Angie whined and contemplated the situation. Then giggling she stood and puckered her lips for her daddy to kiss her. Frank gave her a gentle rub on her shoulder along with several kisses.

Dianna reentered the living room and viewed her husband's gentleness and love. She walked over and stood near their daughter and held the winter coat out for her. Angie slipped into it while giggling and signing "happy." Mom gave her little girl a kiss and returned the sign for "happy."

Nana joined them in the room and wants to assist her granddaughter by zipping up her coat. "No, mom, let Angie do it herself please." Frank's mom steps back to allow Angie the task of zipping up her coat. She did not say a word but stayed right near and watched her granddaughter with her mother signed the spoken words, "Angie, you zip coat."

After several attempts she completed the task of zipping her own coat and proudly signed to all of them "happy." Then dad signed "happy" and mom signed "thank you," while Angie's grandparents stood by and Nana clapped and Papa smiled.

The grandparents each in turn said their good-byes to their youngest granddaughter. Nana with tears in her eyes choked back her emotions, hugged Angie and patted her on the back. Then quickly, she stepped aside and walked over to the other end of the room near Amy and placed her arm around her other granddaughter's shoulders. Papa, a quiet man as usual, held Angie's face within his hands. For a few seconds he looked at her then placed a gentle kiss upon her cheek. Angie clutched at her favorite red purse that sister gave her with mouth agape, chuckled and giggled up at her Papa and signed "happy".

Immediately she turned and signed to everyone "car" while still giggling, proceeded to the back door as if it were another family outing. Parents, sister and grandparents followed her into the kitchen with the family dog close behind.

Nana handed Dianna her coat and helped her to quickly slip it on. In return for the help she smiled back at Nana and said nervously, as she walked toward the back door.

"Hopefully, she'll stay this way until we get her there." She remarked to Nana about Angie's seemingly acceptable serenity.

No sooner those words were spoken, Angie had dropped to her knees and refused to walk any further. Mom placed herself in front of her daughter. She than signed "stand up!" Calmly she stood up and began slowly to walk towards the door that her father held opened for them. Angie although took her sweet old time as always when leaving the house.

Frank told Amy to go ahead and get into the truck. Without a word and huddled in her high school jacket from the cold air, she obeyed and climbed into the back seat. Amy blinked back her tears, and she did not look in either direction towards her parents, but instead simply turned her head and stared out the other side window.

From around the corner of the house, a hardy gust of wind made Dianna shiver in her heavy winter coat. She looked up and took note of the gloomy, gray November sky. Cynically thinking to her self, "how appropriate for this day."

Slowly one by one Angie came down the back steps jaunting down the walkway to the truck. She paused and looked at her belongings that were neatly packed in the truck bed. For a fleeting moment a confused expression passed across her face.

Not wanting his daughter to get further upset at seeing her things, Frank guided her toward the truck door and signed, "help you get in." After being assisted by her father, she joined her big sister. Hesitantly and without saying a word to no one, Frank looked over at his wife before he climbed into the front seat.

He backed slowly out of their drive way. His wife saw Nana and Papa standing at the back door. Nervously she waved goodbye to them. They looked so vulnerable and sad that their daughter-in-law looks the other way. For several minutes Angie's mother stared out the passenger window without really seeing anything. A cold shiver that came from somewhere deep within suddenly caused Dianna to shake uncontrollably as her hand reached to adjust the heat vent on the dashboard.

"Are you cold, Di? You want me to turn the heat up?"

***

"No, it's alright. I think it's just me." She answered, noticing the time on the dashboard clock.

12

GIGGLES
"Frank, are we going to be late? Maybe we should have left earlier?"

✳✳✳

"No, it will be alright. We will get there, there's plenty of time,' he answered.

Throughout most of the drive, dad, mom and their oldest daughter remained silent, lost in their very own personal thoughts. Frank trapped within his own feelings of the years about what he didn't do in order to help make things better for his family. The circumstances given to him in life were out of his control. Amy still young and immature to fully understand, comprehend and want to accept decisions that her parents had made for her little sister. Dianna sat motionless and burdened with feelings of guilt, emptiness and defeated of the past twelve years. Thoughts about her family 's life of what could have been vanished; and instead replaced by yesterday visions of what were.

In the rear seat sat Angie giggling for only God knew of her own thoughts.

IF ONLY...

"What's wrong, Di?" Frank asked suddenly sitting upright in the chair next to his wife's hospital bed. He had been keeping a vigil while he held her hand. The two of them had been in the maternity ward for some time awaiting the birth of their second child. They spent passing the time together with small talk about Amy and her soon to be brother or sister. The young couple had shared other stories, important events and even some laughter over past experiences. But the talk and laughter seemed to fade when Frank felt a pressure given to his hand and the blank expression on his wife's face. A second time he had asked his wife as he sat closer to her bedside. "Something wrong?"

***

"No, not really, but I think something or someone is starting. She answered with a nervous laugh to her anxious husband. "My sheets feel wet, I do believe my water may have broke." She said, giving him a smile. "Maybe this is it!" She responded very excitedly while checking under the single bed sheet. "At least this could signify maybe it won't be false labor like three weeks ago. Oh God, please let this mean the baby is finally coming."

The young couple looked at each other and chuckled over the strange happening that took place back when they thought it was truly the time for labor. They shared their brief moment of amusement about that funny day and how disappointedly it had all turned out. Besides they thought after all it was the second time around and one should know a little bit more on labor pain.

Concern about his wife's present condition the husband quickly jumped up from his chair and began to questioned jittery. "Did it hurt? Are you in any pain? Di, are you all right? You need me to get the nurse now?"

***

"No, not really. Will you stop and listen!" Feeling exasperated she muttered out loud, Oh Lord, please, help me."

***

"What! What do you want me to do?" He asked impatiently.

***

"Frank, just sit down and give me a minute. I'm all right. I'm not in any excruciating pain this very second. Please, can you allow me to tell you something?"

***

"Di, what do you have to tell me?"

***

"It just felt kind of strange, sort of a different feeling than before, but it has been a few years since that happened. It's just hard to remember back right now. Listen, will you please, press the call button for me because my gown and bedding feel quite uncomfortable." Frank had to bend somewhat forward in his chair to push in the call light that was attached to the side bed rail. While waiting for the nurse's assistance, Dianna started talking and comparing about the first experience of her water breaking. She tried to get more situated in the bed to be more comfortable. Glancing over at her husband she said, "wasn't the same sensation for me, I don't know, unlike the first time around. It's just hard for me to put into the right words. Maybe because this time I'm not up walking the halls, you know, I mean like it was the time with Amy. Remember Frank? How I left a trail in the hallway. Oh, the feeling of it trickling down my legs, gee I was so embarrassed. My first time around to have a baby, God, I didn't know what to expect. *Even right now, I really don't know what to expect with this baby.* Oh God, Frank, it's a feeling I have been carrying within me for such a long time."

***

"Di, come on, you know that no two pregnancies and labors are going to be the same."

***

"I know, I know, it's just that this pregnancy. I can't seem to shake this odd feeling." She said emotionally. "Being pregnant with little Amy, somehow it was all different for me. Even my labor with her, the long eighteen hours of it! I'll never forget that day!"

***

"I sure can't forget that day. It was the longest eighteen hours of my life!" Cried Frank.

✳✳✳

"What do you mean? Longest hours of your life! I was the one in the bed rolling back and forth with my fanny hanging out, and you hollering at me to cover up! She said, a little flabbergasted at his remark.

✳✳✳

"Well, yes, all right now. But I too was going through something hard and difficult."

✳✳✳

"Oh really? What was that?" His wife answered with a questioning look upon her face.

✳✳✳

"Going without a cigarette for a long time." He replied.

✳✳✳

"Well you could have stepped out for a cigarette. Why didn't you?"

✳✳✳

"But I didn't want to leave you." He said, as he gave his wife's hand a small squeeze.

✳✳✳

"Gee Frank, you're such a martyr! What a sacrifice you made." She said sarcastically as she turned her head away to look down at her right hand that rested upon the sheet. Then slowly picking up her head to look into the eyes of a truly good man. She stared at her husband and gave him a tender, loving smile and said, "thank you for sacrificing again. Our second baby, I love you."

The young married couple's intimate moment was interrupted by a sound of an approaching nurse outside their door. She hurriedly rushed into the room to answer the left on call light. The middle age woman showed some signs of being stressed and tired, but at the same time looking rather happy and excited about something. The nurse looked straight at them and announced, "we have another mom down the hall, she is getting closer to deliver. Now young lady, how are you doing?" as she approached the side of the bed.

"Well, I think my water broke. My bedding feels pretty wet like someone popped a water balloon." She said with a nervous laugh.

Frank stood up and moved away from his wife's bedside so the nurse could get a closer look as she removed the sheet. He walked to the foot of the bed and stood there with his arms folded and crossed over his chest. His wore several expressions, one of being concern, impatient and a little mirth. "Well did my wife wet the bed? Is this a good sign?" Frank asked.

"Yes, to both of your questions." She chuckled. Then looking at her patient, she questioned if there were any pain or contractions while she had been busy down the hall with the others. Dianna reported that there was some pain before and after her water had broken, while watching her husband standing and swaying slightly from side to side. She altered her glance back to the nurse and asked if everything was all right. "Yes, I think you are coming along fine, I'll go and get someone to examine you, so we can get a closer look how things are progressing here. I'll also be back with some fresh linens for the bed."

After the nurse exited quickly from the room Frank rejoined his wife at her bedside. He stood there for some length of time and with his left hand slightly rubbed her arm while with his other hand gently stroking her long dark hair. He felt weary, uneasy and really didn't know what else to say at that precise moment. Also he noticed that she was quiet with him and wondered if something else was wrong because both of her hands were gripping the sheet tightly and her head was lowered making it impossible for him to see her face.

"Oh Frank!" She moaned suddenly as a sharp twinge grabbed at her abdomen.

***

"What's wrong?" he asked as the movements of his hands stopped.

***

"Just a slight, bad pain, that's all." his wife responded.

***

"You going to be alright?" He asked with concern.

"I'm fine Pumpkin," she murmured using her favorite nick-named for him. One that was given shortly after they first started going together. "It's to be expected, comes you know with the labor. Besides the pain is beginning to let up, so it's not too bad right now. I'm beginning to breathe somewhat easier now. Gee, I forgot how that pain was supposed to feel. It's all coming back, only God knows just how hard and long my labor will be."

"Let's hope and pray that it won't be that long." Frank commented as he stepped back and looked at his wife.

"Frank, did I ever tell you what Doctor Swind said to me at my last appointment? Not with this pregnancy but before I went into labor with Amy?"

"What Di, I'm not certain what you're talking about?

***

"Well, I was real concerned about how bad the labor pains were going to be. And he told me that it would feel nothing more than if I would happen to eat a sour green apple and get a bad belly ache."

***

"In that case you must had eaten a bushel barrel with Amy," he said jokingly.

Just then as the two of them were laughing over the remark, his wife had felt another intense pain joined with more of the releasing of body fluids absorbing into the bedding.

"Frank, I think you better look for someone!"

***

"Why? Are you having more pain, is it time?"

***

"I don't know, but the pain is getting worse and I will drown if this bed should get any wetter. I guess it's my water again. I hurt, feel miserable and very uncomfortable." She tried to pull herself up into a half sitting position by grabbing onto the side bed rail. He watched and refused to move and just stood looking down at his wife with a concerned expression on his face.

"I'm alright, don't worry, honey. Just get someone please to check on my progress and to help me."

Before Frank could even try to walk out of the room, he took a few steps closer to the bed and bent down to give his wife a kiss and said, "I love you, don't move, stay right there and I'll be back, I'll find that lady, Di!" Her nervous and excited husband finally exits the labor room.

With a deep sigh of anticipation Dianna laid back in her wet bed to contemplate about her husband's words and the present, weary moments. Her eyes were closed and her mind was saying," there is no other place to go, I'm right where I should be, waiting for my labor to become stronger, awaiting the birth of my second baby. All those months thinking, wondering about all the unexpected happenings. Waiting for this day to approach and give me the final moment of truth. But first I have to get through my labor. Oh God, can you really hear what is inside my head? God, You do know that everyday I have been praying and begging to let my baby be all right! Now here I am, waiting just waiting. Dear God, I wonder, shouldn't my pain be getting stronger? Will my labor be like the first time? But so far the baby has been quiet or still. I'm scared. I'm all giggles on the outside, but frightened on the inside. Why God, have I had this uneasy feeling that something is wrong ever since the accident when I was eight weeks pregnant?" She continued to lay with her head upon the pillow, tears quietly flowing down her cheeks and her eyes kept closed, as if somehow she could shut away that horrible day from her memory. Once more she heard those painful words lifted to Him. "Please God, let my baby be all right. Let me be worried for nothing! If only certain incidents had never happened. Then I could erase this fear and uncertainty within me. If only that accident in my kitchen seven months ago never happened. If only."

***

"Momma needs to get you some cereal now, Amy. Lets place you in your high chair and move you over by the table, so I can get into the cupboard." Dianna said, as she gently slid her daughter into the green and white flowered highchair. It was given as a shower gift by little Amy's grandmother.

***

"Urnch, urnch", a happy little toddler smiled up at her mommy while trying to point at the kitchen cabinets.

***

"Yes, momma will get down your favorite bowl as soon as I lock your tray in place. Wouldn't want my baby to fall out and get hurt."

***

"Urnch, urnch," again responded Amy to her mommy using her so-called and only word.

***

"First let mommy go over and open the window to get some fresh air." Said Dianna, as she parted the reddish-orange curtains with earth tones of colored fringes that hung at the old fashioned long window of the rented duplex. She took note of the early June summer morning. Dew drops sparkling on the next- door neighbor's flower petals. "Amy, I think it will be a nice day for a walk," as she continued to stare out the window at the neighbor's assorted flowered bed.

Squealing with delight and clapping her small, delicate hands, Amy responded once again with her word, "urnch, urnch!"

***

"Oh, you are so cute. Momma just loves you to pieces," Dianna said, as she turned from the window and walked over to her daughter sitting happily and patiently in the high chair. The child's mommy bent forward and tenderly placed a kiss upon the silky, blond curls. She then stepped back and looked adoringly at her sweet little daughter. So precious with big brown eyes and the perfect doll like body wearing her parents' favorite pink and yellow bunny print sleepwear. "Amy, you are such a good baby. Although your mommy remembers times when you were always moving," as she patted the front of her stomach, "so impatient to be born it seemed. I wonder if your little brother or sister will be just as active. Mommy remembers the very first time that you moved in me," as she gently finger tapped Amy's nose.

***

"Urnch?" Amy looked up at her mother with a beautiful baby smile.

***

"Yes honey, I'll always remember that first time," she told herself. Dianna resumed with those heart warm thoughts of her mother and spoke them out loud to her daughter. She walked back over to the kitchen window to continue her story. "Your grandma, my mommy, was with me. It was around two in the morning and your daddy had just brought me home from work to grandma and grandpa's house. We said our goodnights and daddy went home to your Nana and Papa's house. I, your mommy was getting ready for bed. I started to feel an uncomfortable twinge in my tummy. It frightened me so that your mommy couldn't go to sleep. So I went downstairs to wake up your grandma. I thought something was wrong. But grandma got out of bed and took me into the living room and calmed me down. We sat together on the couch while grandma explained to me that it was probably the first time I felt life with you. I'll never forget that night. I was too scared and upset to go back to bed, so your grandma, my mommy spent the night with me on the couch. She made me feel so safe, that I knew if something were to happen she would be there. "You know Amy," she said and turned to face the child in the highchair. The child's mother kept speaking but more to her self about that particular and precious moment that was shared between two women, of one who gave her wisdom, love and support to one who really needed to hear the truly womanly experiences. "I think it was that night honey, that I felt the closet ever to my mother."

Dianna moved away from the kitchen window and walked over and stood in front of the highchair. She stared down lovingly at her baby girl. Silently she pondered while momentarily became lost in her reflecting thoughts. Remembering how hard it was for her parents, to deal with the fact that their youngest daughter was unwed, pregnant and still in high school. From that moment on, she realized that her mother wasn't angry or disappointed with the young girl anymore. Dianna's mother had accepted the pregnancy before marriage with forgiveness and love. "All because of that night and you!" Dianna exclaimed touching tenderly the cheek of little Amy.

The child's mommy stooped down in front of the chair and said to her baby girl, "you know Amy, your dad and I are very lucky to have parents that have been so supportive of us and very proud to have you for their granddaughter! But, who wouldn't be? You're so cute!" Mom said, as she tapped the delicate little nose.

Feeling inpatient with her mother's reminiscing and eager to eat, Amy started to hit the tray top with her little hands crying, "urnch!"

"Oh Amy, I'm so sorry. Momma got carried away, didn't I?" Dianna chuckled as she walked quickly back over to the kitchen cabinets above the sink.

She reached up to open one of the cupboard doors that contained the dishes, bowls and other items that were used daily by her family. With both hands she pulled opened the enclosures, when unexpectedly without warning of a sound or noise of any kind, a white blur flashed before her eyes. In a reflex motion of Dianna's right arm had flown up to protect her face. A dull "thud" hit the right palm of her hand as several large, white Flintstones glass bowls came crashing down into the sink and onto the counter top with glass flying in all directions. Startled and numbed, Dianna stood and trembled as she tried to focus down at the shattered array of milky glass that was once a gift from her mother-in-law, now scattered upon the counter top, sink and floor.

Quickly she remembered Amy sitting in the highchair and spun around to make sure that her little one was unharmed. Her daughter's eyes were wide opened in a startled expression without any implication of sound from what had just occurred in the kitchen. Dianna rushed over to where Amy was sitting. She nervously prayed and checked her little one carefully all over. Amy's mother kept praying and hoping while she continued to make sure that none of the glass flew to hit her precious baby. She was all right! "Thank You, God," Dianna prayed out loud that her daughter was unharmed by the incident.

Now standing in shock and glancing around at her kitchen and looking down at the floor, so covered with pieces of shattered glass, she noticed blood splattered on the floor from the cabinets to Amy's highchair.

"Where did this blood come from?" She asked herself somewhat dazedly. "Oh my God, what happened?" Dianna cried.

Quickly she started to examine herself. Looking down first at her right hand because of a burning throb she felt that began to pulse up her arm. Blood was flowing from a wide, open and deep looking gash at the base of the thumb.

The next few moments were filled with panic and desperation, as she stood stunned and frozen with fear in the kitchen watching the blood run down off her hand forming a small puddle at her feet.

"Help! Help me!" She called out in hope the upstairs landlord would hear and come to her rescue; for Dianna was paralyzed with fright and seemed incapable of any movement.

Crying hysterically she screamed again. "Help me! Oh God, someone please help me!" little Amy now frightened by what had just happened to her mother begins to whimper.

"Amy, don't cry!" Her mom pleaded, trying to compose herself so as not to frighten her child further. "Mamma needs to get some help, honey I'll be right back!" Dianna rushed to the back door. Throwing the door open, she ran up the back stairway leaving a trail of blood and screaming, "Connie, help me! Oh God, Jim and Connie please help me"

Their landing door is suddenly opened by Jim, who upon seeing his tenant predicament and all the blood with haste turns back around into their kitchen grabbing a dish towel. Jim applied pressure with the towel to the wound and quickly wrapped it around the hand and wrist.

His wife Connie hearing the frightened commotion entered the kitchen and asked, "Jim, what's wrong? What are you doing?" Then seeing Dianna's ashen colored face, Connie inquired to both of them. "Jim, oh my God, Dianna what happened?"

Crying too hysterically to answer her, Connie's question was interrupted by her husband. "Hand me another towel, Connie." Jim ordered quickly as he led Dianna into their kitchen and settled her down in a chair near the kitchen table.

"What happened to her Jim?" Handing him another clean dry towel she asked again.

***

"I don't know Connie, but she has a very deep cut here. She's losing a lot of blood and should be taken to the hospital."

Still sobbing Dianna tried to gain control enough to explain to both of them what happened. "The bowls fell out of the cup board," She blurted out grasping for breath. "I was getting Amy's cereal bowl, when they just fell down on me. I didn't even feel them hit me. I just opened the cabinet door and down they came. There's glass everywhere! Thank God, Amy wasn't sitting anywhere near, when all this happened!"

***

"Dianna, where is Amy?" Inquired Connie.

***

"Oh my God, Connie she's down stairs in the kitchen by herself," Dianna cried uncontrollably.

***

"Don't worry, you calm down now, everything will be all right." Said Jim. "Connie, go down stairs and bring Amy up here, and I will drive Dianna to the hospital. She's definitely going to need some stitches in her hand."

"Amy hasn't had any breakfast yet," Dianna mentioned to Connie, as she started toward the back stairway. "Be careful, there's glass all over the floor. God, please, I forgot about my baby, let my Amy be all right!"

"Don't worry, I'll feed Amy and then the boys can watch her for me when I go back down and clean up the glass." Connie replied.

"Thanks Connie, for helping me with Amy, but I can take care of the kitchen when I get back."

***

"No, let Connie do that, because you won't be in any condition," said Jim, removing the car keys from the rack on the wall. Then he assisted Dianna down the back stairway, for she was still very shaken and weak from the shock and loss of blood.

The short ride to the hospital was spent quietly; Jim concerned with getting quick medical attention for his renter. Dianna was still in a daze and continued to stare down at the blood soaked towel that she was holding firmly around her throbbing hand. The pain was so intense as it burned its way up the arm, causing her to fight back the tears.

Upon reaching the hospital emergency unit, Dianna was immediately noticed and was quickly ushered into an examining room by a hospital staff. The nurse told her to lie down on the small, narrow table. She unwrapped the towels from her patient's hand and began to examine in order to cleanse the wound.

"Would you like a blanket?" The nurse asked, noticing that Dianna was shaking.

***

"Yes please, I'm so cold." Dianna answered. As she waited for the nurse to return with the blanket, she bravely took a chance to look at her uncovered wound. It looked horrible! Already distorted with swelling and discoloration. Blood was still seeping from the gaping crevice that half encircled the base of the thumb. It looked to Dianna as if the thumb was half severed, lying there at an awkward angle. Between the excruciating pain and the ugliness of the hand, she could no longer hold back the tears.

"Turn your head toward the wall, honey," instructed the nurse upon returning with the blanket that she placed over her patient's trembling body. "The doctor will be in here soon."

For the next few minutes while they waited for the doctor, the nurse stayed with her patient standing at the bedside and soothingly rubbing Dianna's forehead to calm her anxiety. Lying there with her eyes closed, she heard the soft footsteps as the hospital's attending physician entered the room.

"What happened here?" He inquired, beginning to examine the hand.

***

"My glass bowls fell out of the cup board on me and cut my hand," she answered, turning her head back to face the physician.

Without saying anything further to the patient, he instructed the nurse to bring the necessary items that he would need to care for her hand. Dianna winced with pain as he started to prep her hand.

"I will now numb your hand, so I can stitch you up. Please hold still. You will feel a slight prick. It shouldn't hurt you too much."

The physician tried to be gentle as he administered the nova cane and that she barely felt the needle; in comparison to the excruciating, burning pain still throbbing up her arm.

Within moments Dianna became aware of a warm tingling feeling spreading through her hand that replaced the throbbing pain. Dianna once again closed her eyes as he began stitching. For several minutes he worked in silence. She could feel some tugging and pinching from the sutures. Finally, she turned her head to see if he was almost finished.

"Just a few more stitches," as he answered his patient's unspoken question. "You were lucky that you didn't completely sever your thumb."

***

"Will I be alright?"

✳✳✳

"Oh yes, your hand should heal just fine," he replied.

✳✳✳

"No, I mean will I be alright? I'm pregnant."

Halting his suturing in mid-air, he looked up at Dianna and asked, "How far along are you?"

✳✳✳

"I just found out that I am about eight to ten weeks pregnant." She answered in a mousy voice.

He stared at his patient for a few seconds. Then without answering he quietly resumed his suturing...

"NANNY"

"Doctor Swynds, do you two have to sit there?"

***

"Well, yes, Dianna. We're waiting for the baby."

***

"But do you two have to sit right there?"

***

"Where would you like us to sit, Dianna?" He asked with a "who care where I sit" grin and a quick glance toward his assistant.

"Anywhere but there!" I said, sighing deeply as I lay my head back down on the delivery table. Ignoring my question, they resume their conversation sitting at my feet. "It's easy for you to think nothing about it," I think to myself. You're not the one with your legs up in stirrups and your knees spread wide apart for anyone passing by to look at." Dianna thought to herself. "I just hope this little covering doesn't shift in any direction."

Feeling not only embarrassed of her delivery position, but also uncomfortable from the strange numbing effect of the saddle that had just been administered within the last few minutes, Dianna started to giggle, while saying quietly to herself, as she lay half motionless on the small table. "You would think it was my first time."

Nervously her fingers fidget with the hem of the hospital sheet that is draped across her body. All around there is commotion as the delivery room staff scurries about doing their individual tasks. Dianna's thoughts turned to her husband, thinking how anxious and cute he looked standing in the hallway as his young wife was rolled toward the delivery room.

"I wonder how Frank is doing? Hope he's not waiting by himself. He gets so nervous and upset when he's anxious, worrying about me. I wish he could be in here with me. I could use his comforting support right now. I don't like going through this by myself. I feel all alone even though there are other people in here." Occasionally, someone would come over to check on the patient's progress, but it only adds to the mixed feeling of being apart from it, when one should really feel part of it. Dianna thinks to herself, "We're all probably thinking the same thing, when will this baby get here? Why did my labor have to stop? Everything was moving along just fine until they gave me that darn saddle. Wonder what time it is anyways? Oh God, I feel like this will never end. How much longer? If I could just see what time it is?"

Searching the room for a clock, Dianna finally locates one on the wall behind her. Although trying to catch the time becomes a bit awkward because of the bodily position upon the narrow table. The upper half of her body cooperated with movement, but the lower section seemed quite of any immobilization. In order to view the given time, she had to awkwardly bend her head backward to get a better look at the clock that hung on the delivery room wall behind her.

"It's 7:50 A.M., I've been in here for forty minutes? Gee, it feels like it's been hours!" Dianna exclaimed out loud. She started her giggling again. Thinking how funny this all must appear, when suddenly the two doctors got up from where they were sitting, said something to one of the staff and left without mentioning anything to the young woman who laid half immovable, ready and hoping to give birth. "Well! "She chuckled out loud. "They must have finally got tired of the view. Does this mean that my baby and I are on hold?"

"Be patient Dianna. Shouldn't be much longer." Said one of the delivery room nurses who walked over to stand at the side of the table. She looked down at the frightened and very nervous girl, with gentle eyes and a warm, supportive smile. "Is this your first?"

"No, my second."

***

"Sometimes the second one might take a little longer too. Just be patient dear."

***

"Don't tell me that, tell my doctor. He just walked out." Dianna said giggling.

She laughs and pats her patient's hand and walks away. Minutes that seem like hours keep ticking by as the awaiting mother laid there deep in thought about the birth of her second baby.

"Very soon now Amy, I hope mommy will give you a little brother or sister." She whispers. Silently, she prays, "God, let my baby be okay. Please give us another healthy baby like Amy."

Although deep down somewhere within Dianna's heart, is this nagging fear that something is desperately wrong that still linger there. "All these months I have carried this feeling with me. Is it because I have hardly felt any movement of life? The most I have ever felt was like a small butterfly fluttering around in me. And that little stirring didn't start until after the car accident with my girlfriend Jenna and I were in when we were both four months along. Oh God, I wonder."

***

"I wonder if our husbands have miss us?" Said Jenna, looking over at Dianna and smiling as she is driving them back to the apartment from a brief shopping trip.

"Won't they be surprised we are back so soon," Dianna remarked. As she adjusted her seat belt for better comfort and than glanced over at her high school friend. "If I know Frank, he's probably worrying about how much money I have spent tonight."

"No way, I think our two guys are still glued to the television watching that football game. You know, they probably don't really miss us because of the game."

"Oh how true Jenna, that explains why you and I are both pregnant at the same time. There weren't any football games on in May."

The two best friends were both laughing as Jenna came to a stop at the red light. For the late hour into the evening the traffic seemed very heavy at this particular intersection.

"Oh Dianna, have you seen any of the girls from school lately?"

***

"No, Jenna, I guess my life is pretty wrapped up with being a wife and mother. How about you, have you run into any of the girls from school?"

"Yeah, a few but you know, they 're surprised I got married so soon from high school. But we didn't want to wait and it was fine with my dad."

"Let's face it Jenna, you just wanted to follow in my footsteps." Dianna said. "At least you waited till after you graduated from school."

"Oh Dianna, don't be so hard on yourself. So what if you and Frank got married before you two graduated. It happened, you got pregnant, big deal. So you shocked a lot of people. But you both did the right thing, the two of you got married, finished school and besides you have a beautiful little daughter." Jenna said, trying to comfort her friend.

"You are right about me shocking a lot of people. My parents, his parents, family, school friends and I don't want to forget the nuns. After all I was at one time going to become a nun. I'm sure being pregnant in my senior year didn't give the school a good name."

Jenna looked over at her passenger, "Dianna, somehow I can't quite see you as a nun. You're better off married to Frank and having Amy. Besides just look at us, we're two old happily married girls and getting big!"

"Yes my friend, you can say that again."

***

Both young women were laughing about body weight gain when it dawned on Dianna. "Jenna, have we forgotten how we will look in the next couple of months from now? Soon you and I will very much take on another new and bigger appearance."

"You're so right about that! My obstetrician has already told me to be careful in gaining too much weight too soon." Jenna answered looking over at her friend just as she is making a left hand turn in front of an oncoming car.

"Jenna! Look out! He's coming at us!" Dianna screamed as she noticed the approaching headlights.

"Oh God no!" Shrieked Jenna as the two cars collided.

***

Screeching tires and a loud bang are the sounds Dianna heard upon the impact. Her body was thrown side ways against the inside of her friend's car door. Seconds later and dazed she was aware of far away voices descending on them. Dianna became aware of people standing around the car peering in at her and Jenna. She could hear her friend talking but unaware of what she was saying. Jenna's passenger felt numb as she started to cry while gasping for air. Dianna took in a deep breath quickly and felt a strange feeling within her abdomen. Panic and fear started to register as the tears rolled swiftly down her face. She finally collected herself enough to look over at her friend who seemed very distraught at what had just taken place. The driver seemed to be extremely confused and perhaps in the state of shock.

"Jenna, are you alright?" Dianna concerned for her friend.

***

"I think so, oh Dianna what happened?" Cried Jenna.

***

"The car came right at us as you were turning, all I saw were the head lights coming towards us. It happened so fast, the bright lights and the loud noise. I sure hope that we will be al l right! I was bumped around pretty good. How about you? How are you feeling?"

"I don't know. I guess everything is all right. How about you?"

***

"Jenna, my stomach hurts a little, it feels just a little strange. I think that we was tossed around good."

***

It is then that the two young women noticed a couple of men getting out of their car that hit them. They ran over to the driver's side of the car. Jenna hopefully appeared to Dianna to be uninjured for her friend was rolling down the car window to speak to the other party.

"Are you girls alright? The two men anxiously inquired for they had fright and concern written all over their faces.

"We're both pregnant! We're both pregnant!" Hysterically screamed Jenna.

***

Stunned at her outburst they stood there starring in at the two so - called pregnant women. Jenna continued to babble on to them about the accident and the need to call their husbands while her passenger just sits there quietly sobbing with her head bent forward. One of the two guys offered to call the police and an ambulance. As he left a small crowd began to form around the area. Another stranger approached the vehicle to inquired if anyone was seriously injured or if he could be of some assistance. He asked if the young ladies could remove themselves from the car, after someone had mentioned to him that they were both with child. Hearing that the women thought they could get out of Jenna's car, the older gentleman assisted them toward a small coffee shop, a short distance away from the accident. He was kind enough to stay until the police had arrived. In the meantime Jenna was uncontrollably gesturing to anyone who would listen about how the accident wasn't her fault. Her actions seemed wild and melodramatic to others around her, but to Dianna it was Jenna who was reacting from shock. Jenna's friend watched on while she sat on a nearby chair trying to keep calm. All she could think about at that moment if anything had happened to her unborn child. Dianna felt alone, frightened, confused and worried about how they should contact their husbands. Jenna had to be the one to place the call to her house for her friend wasn't capable of remembering the number. After several long moments of commotion Dianna finally caught her friend's attention.

Jenna nervously phoned her husband and explained that they had been in an auto accident. Worried and anxious Dan arrived with Frank before the police and ambulance since the accident happened nearby their apartment. Dan shot questions at Jenna while Frank held his toddler daughter in his arms. Jenna's husband wanted to know how and what had happened since she was driving. His wife tried to explain that it had just happened so fast. Dan stood and listened with his arm around his wife's shoulder. Meanwhile Frank continued to hold Amy as he listened and stood next to Dianna. Both parents were aware as to not upset their small daughter.

The police joined by the other driver and his passenger all conjugated into the small shop to talk with Jenna and Dianna. Both women took turns to explain the incident and what they thought might have happened earlier. Jenna tried her best to recall how she had the left blinker on and saw the green arrow for her to proceed to make the left turn. The police agreed that her statement was correct because the other driver admitted that he was definitely in the wrong. The policemen suggested immediately to the young women to be examined by medical staff since they both were pregnant. Vitals were taken, questions were asked and some oxygen was given for breathing discomfort en route to the hospital.

Upon their arrival both women were ushered into separate examining rooms. Dan along with Frank and little Amy tried to wait patiently in the waiting room. Jenna was examined first and later was able to join her husband. Dianna was kept in the room longer because the nurse had a little trouble getting a fetal heartbeat with the stethoscope. Later Dianna was surprised to find out that her friend was given nothing to take before leaving the hospital. For Dianna was given a purple pill, the emergency room stated to calm the patient.

***

"Don't bear down, Dianna! Your doctor is not in the room yet! Wait!"

✲✲✲

"I can't wait! I didn't tell him to leave in the first place! Get Doctor Swynds back in here because this baby is not waiting!" Dianna laughed as one of delivery room staff quickly exited.

"Well little one, all these months you've been so quiet, I guess now this is your time to make yourself known." Dianna quietly whispered to her unborn child, as the delivery became more apparent.

"Dianna, It sounds like you are ready to deliver. This little one gave us a waiting period." Doctor Swynds condescendingly remark as he re-entered the delivery room.

"Hurry up Doc! This time stay in here! Don't even try to ask me to wait either, this baby is ready and so am I!" Dianna demanded nervously between giggles.

Even though the saddle blocked the labor pains, Dianna was still aware of some pressure as the baby continued it's downward movement through the birth canal. But for some unexplained reason she kept on giggling and laughing. At one point Dianna actually thought she could hear the clip-clipping sound as the doctor performed the episiotomy. Doctor Swynds then gave a final push on her stomach. With a giant rush of relief, Dianna's baby was born.

"It's another girl Dianna." Doctor Swynds proudly proclaimed as he handled the new baby daughter to a nurse who immediately took the infant to the other side of the delivery room.

"Is she alright?" Dianna asked, for there were no sounds coming from her daughter. Is my baby alright?" She asked again.

"Why isn't she crying? Isn't she suppose to be crying, Doc? What's wrong with her? She's so quiet!"

"Some babies don't always cry right away." Replied Doctor Swynds. "That doesn't mean there's something wrong. She'll be just fine."

"I want to see her, now! Please!"

✲✲✲

"You will Dianna, but right now she's being examine, they will weigh her, clean and all the other important factors concerning the welfare of the infant."

"Alright Doctor, but do me a favor, will you? Just check my baby girl all over and make sure that everything is fine with her." Dianna pleadingly asked, as he continued with the post pardon procedures.

"Now, now, don't start worrying. She'll be checked over good. Let's calm your self down. No need to get upset. You've been doing just great so far. In fact, I believe that you are my very first patient that giggled her baby right out of her."

Dianna's attention was only focused on listening intently for any little sounds that would perhaps come from her baby. But all she heard were hushed voices mixed with other delivery room noises. Than like a quick rush it seemed to her, someone immediately took hold of the cart and wheeled the mother out of the delivery area. Dianna was placed into a room without even a chance to see or hold her baby. Some time later after being settled and all the necessities being done to the patient, her husband was allowed to visit. He quietly entered the room and walked over to his wife's bedside for not to disturbed her in case she was sleeping. But he was surprised to see that his wife was not resting, instead she stared straight at the wall. Hearing the approaching sounds of someone entering the room, Dianna turned her head to look at the restless man with hands in his pant pockets, cigarette packet nestled above in the shirt and a face that revealed tiredness, concern and most of all his love to the young woman. "Were you able to see her Frank? I haven't seen our daughter yet!"

"Yes, Di. She's just as beautiful as Amy but only smaller."

✳✳✳

"Frank, are you disappointed that I didn't give you a son?"

✳✳✳

"No, Di. Don't be so silly!"

✳✳✳

"But I was so sure that it was going to be a boy, we could have named after you." Jokingly said. "Well maybe one Frank is meant to be. It's all this world can handle. Honey, we still have to give our new daughter a name. We'll have to pick one from the few we did select."

"Di, there's time, you and I will find just the right name for her. Besides now I have three beautiful girls to take care of." He said leaning over his wife to place a gentle kiss.

Pulling up a chair, he sat quietly next to the bed and held her hand for he knew she was tired but did not realized his wife's mental status of being drained physically and mentally. Also exhausted from the whole delivery experience, one so entirely different from her first. The saddle that was administered before was wearing off so she thought, leaving a slight tingling sensation as feeling was slowly and gradually returning to the lower part of her body. He lingered at her bedside for about an hour just making some small talk.

"Why don't you go home Frank and rest for a while? You look as tired as I feel. Besides honey, they said they won't bring the baby in until later."

"Are you sure? You don't mind?"

***

"Yes, it's fine. So go home and spend some time with Amy and tell her about her new baby sister and that I love her. Just make sure you come back this evening and be with me. Then maybe we can decide on a name for our new daughter. How does that sound?"

Giving her hand a squeeze, he kissed his wife several times and said, "I love you and thank you."

"I love you too Frank. I'll see you this evening and, oh, tell Nana and Papa I said thanks for taking care of Amy."

Dianna upon being alone found some time to reason with her self that everything was fine just like the doctor had told her. Perhaps she was thinking about too many unnecessary things that were clouding her thinking. Finally she would allow time to ease her fears, troubled mind and tired body to relax and rest. But she soon found out rest was not going to be easy to come by. A comfortable position in the bed she needed first, but reality told her that laying flat for a while because of the injection given before delivery. If she wanted to avoid any headaches or other complications one had to obey the hospital instructions. Instead Dianna closed her eyes and listened to all the sounds that surrounded her room. Her right fingers played with her wedding band as her left hand also felt restless against the blanket. For a few minutes she thought rest might enter her body but only feeling more restless physically and mentally. Dianna's mind was preoccupied with too many worries, concerns and unanswered questions. Noises outside her room that seemed to find their way into her space quickly made her eyes open. Lunch was being served or placed upon the bed table.

Without a single word to the patient the young dietician aid set the lunch tray down on the bed next to Dianna's head and simply walked out of the room. It seemed to be a very appetizing lunch from the prone position of the viewer. Fried chicken, mashed potatoes with gravy, drinks and last but not least a vegetable; a side dish of rolling green peas. All of her favorite foods, for Dianna did seem somewhat hungry.

"But how am I going to eat this, when I'm suppose to lay flat on my back?" She murmured.

"I'll just have to push the call button for help." Dianna looked for the call light and discovered it sitting on the nightstand, which was too far from the bed for her to reach. Thinking out loud, "Well looks like I will have to fend for myself. If I am going to eat lunch and someway, somehow I am going to because I am hungry!"

With determination she carefully and slowly reached for the silverware and napkin that was on the tray. She took out the paper napkin and unfolded it to place upon her chest. Next she pulled out the knife from the plastic wrap in order to butter the roll. She tried hard to be neat as possible without making a big mess. The thigh of the chicken had to be attack by her fingers as she tore away at the meat. This method did not appear too difficult when the fork was put to the test for the mash potatoes. The peas that were prepared in their buttery juices in the small round bowl were definitely a different story.

First Dianna tried forking them. Some did manage to stick to the end. To quicken the meal up the spoon took the place of the fork. Big mistake! As she tipped the spoon to accommodate her eating position, the peas spilled out rolling down her neck, chest and bed, never reaching the mouth. "Oh well, they might have looked a pretty green but too hard to eat anyways." She thought. Feeling a little frustrated and laying in her bed surrounded by the peas, she finally gave up. The ice cream for dessert would just have to melt in its container.

"How are we doing with our lunch, Dianna?" Asked a nurse entering the room.

***

"Well, I guess I managed fairly well, if you want to over look the fact I'm surrounded by peas."

***

"Oh, now that's not a very easy way to eat. Looks like you ate and did pretty good though. But you're right from the looks of it, you do have some peas around." She laughed as she began removing the green vegetable from my bed. "If you are finished, I will remove the tray? Then perhaps get you clean up some, you should even try and get some rest."

"How much longer do I have to lay flat here and when do I get to hold my baby?"

***

"In a little while, baby will be brought in for her feeding. Then at that time I will raise the head of your bed. Now that I have you cleaned up and hope there's no more peas under your pillow, you should really try and get some rest before the little one arrives." The nurse tuned and left the room.

Dianna closed her eyes and drifted in and out of a fretful sleep filled with nightmarish images of deceased family members in unfamiliar surroundings devoid of color and light. Except for her dress. The one she was buried in. A simple powder blue dress with white cuff sleeves and collar. She stands out so vividly from amongst the other figures, they are cloaked in misty blurred shadows. Silently they stand in line behind and off to one side of her. Sensing more than seeing, Dianna knew they are her deceased grandparents and an aunt. The very young girl stood there freely without the entrapments of the heavy leg braces that were once a familiar part of her earthly being. Solemnly she beckons with her hand and arm calling out to Dianna.

"Come with me, I want to show you how beautiful it is here. I am so happy."

***

"Nan, I can't come with you right now. I just had another baby! Nan, but I do love you though and miss you so very much. It's just that I'm worried because I think there is something wrong with my baby."

"Dianna, bring your baby and don't worry, she will be taken care of. Please come with me." She mournfully wails.

Nan stood there as she continued her pleading to her sister. In Dianna's dream, suddenly she happens to see their mother. Mother is talking to the faceless apparitions. Dianna unable to make out what the ghostly images are saying, for the spoken words sound mumbled. She tried hard to listen and at the same time she looks even harder to focus on the appearances clouded around the older woman. Dianna thought that she recognized her deceased grandmother, standing there, among the other figures talking to her daughter Alice. Dianna's mother, reached out her hand and placed it within her mother's own hand. Another figure drifted over next to them and ever so gently put her arm around the older woman's shoulder. Than like in slow motion, Dianna's mother moved backwards away from the shrouded appearances and lifted her hand in the mist for a farewell salute. Next she turned to face the daughter. Nan, who was her fifth child who she lost so very young in life at the age of ten.

Dianna continued to witness the exchanged glances and words between her mother and her deceased younger sister. She watched the picture before her as mother and daughter stood there face to face. Dianna could only see the back of her mother, but she was very aware of her sister's glowing face. An angel's face with a warm smile as she directly looked at her earthly mother and repeatedly stated, "I am so happy here!"

Without a single word or motion to the daughter, mom quietly and gently faded away from Dianna's vision. Although her sister Nan continued to stand so straight and firm within her dream, still with the powder blue dress and the white collar and cuffs. Once again Dianna's sister beckoned and she heard her little sister say, "Please come with me. Dianna, please bring your baby and come with me."

A LITTLE VISIT

"Dianna, wake up. You have a little visitor."

❋

"No, no please, I can not go with you." Dianna silently responded to the voice. Than suddenly she was awaked and aware of the surroundings in the hospital room.

"You were sleeping so soundly, but I don't think you will mind this small interruption." The nurse smiles while she cranked up the head of the bed until her patient was almost in a sitting position.

Dianna focused her eyes to the afternoon light in the room. She saw a hospital's bassinet near the foot of the bed. Wrapped in the hospital's baby blankets, the only exposed thing visible to the eye was a small dark haired head with an angel like face, laid Dianna's new born baby daughter, so still and sound asleep.

The excited mom with outstretched arms waiting to hold her second baby daughter. Dianna was taken back to the first time with Amy; excited but apprehensive to hold her first born, who too had a face like an angle with a crown of dark hair.

"Oh my, she is so tiny." Dianna remarked as the nurse gently placed the infant in her arms.

❋

"Yes, she is," acknowledged the nurse. "But I personally prefer smaller babies. They grow up so fast anyways."

❋

The baby's mother looked down at her sleeping daughter and happily announced, "You look just like your big sister Amy, but only smaller."

"Is Amy your only other child?" Asked the nurse.

❋

"Yes, she's our first."

❋

47

"How much did she weigh at birth?" She further inquired as she straightened the bed covers.

***

"Amy weighed eight pounds and three ounces and I think she was twenty-one inches long."

***

"That is a pretty good size for your first, Dianna. Well, let's see what this little one's stats are," she said walking over to the bassinet to read the pink card that was attached. "Six pounds and fifteen ounces and she measures nineteen inches long. That's a perfect size for a little girl. Do you and your husband have a name picked out for her?"

"No, not yet, if we had a boy, we were going to name him after my husband Frank. I was so sure that this time we were going to have a boy, so we didn't really decide on a girl's name. So this evening when daddy comes back to visit us, we are going to choose just the right name for this little one." Dianna said cuddling her baby closely.

"Well, I'll let you two visit for a little while. Is there anything you need before I leave?" She asked.

***

"No, I am just fine now. I have everything I need right here in my arms."

***

Quietly closing the door behind her, the nurse departed and for the next few moments, Dianna just sat there cradling her baby, staring at nothing as once again she was overcome with that uneasy, anxious feeling that something was not right.

The new born baby laid so still, that the baby's mother had to lean closer to the infant's face to listen as her labored breathing came in the form of short, shallow breaths. A stilled like picture of a motionless doll lying in the mother's arms.

Suddenly, Dianna unwrapped her baby from the blankets in an unnatural frenzy. She began to hope and pray to find nothing that would justify her fears. So tiny are the legs and arms, but the little one does have ten little toes and fingers. Gently she picked up the small hands and noticed there were no fingernails or perhaps they are too transparent to see; and her toenails were the very same way. The mother noticed her daughter's skin looked pale and waxen in color. Mom also detected a bluish tint above her baby's lips. Except for the skin coloring, the baby seemed normal, just so tiny, fragile and stilled so sound asleep. With a sigh of relief Dianna wrapped her baby girl back up in the blankets and gently kissed her forehead. Even those facial features looked so delicate.

A soft whisper, "Please wake up my little one" and the baby's mother gave her a slight nudge. "Momma would like to see your eyes." Dianna gently brushed her fingertips across her daughter's forehead and cheeks. That's when she noticed the ear lope. It was pointed, pear shape. She quickly checked the other for a match. Yes, just like her younger sister Nan. This precious gift from God had her Aunt Nan's shaped ear lopes.

A B C

Later, that same day, Frank returned for the evening visit. Unlike today's relaxed hospitals visitation rules, back then, twenty-five some years ago, all visitors were required to check in at the front desk to get a pass card. Visitations were limited to fifteen minutes and only two visitors at a time per patient.

But Frank, with his independent spirit, refused to stop at the front desk and would walk right on past to the elevators. There was one time when he had been stopped by a guard who inquired where he was going; Frank replied that he was on his way up to see his wife and new daughter. The guard reminded him to first check in and get his visitor's pass card. Upon which Frank retorted, "I'm the father! Not the visitor!" He then continued on his way to the elevators.

"Hmmm...Don't you look sexy," he said as he winked at his wife and leaned over her to place a kiss upon her mouth.

"I like what you are wearing Di." He referred to the standard hospital gown.

"Right Pumpkin, I saved this sexy little number especially for this moment with you." She chuckled sarcastically as she returned the kiss.

"I brought you something Di," he said with a wink and a sheepish grin. Frank reached inside the pocket of his black leather coat and he pulled out a small paperback book.

"Remember this?" He asked.

***

"What! No flowers or candy again, Frank?" She pouted.

***

"Break my tradition, besides you're sweet enough and the girls and I are your flowers." Answered Frank.

Taking the book from him, she said, "I do remember this and the evenings we spent with Nana and Papa in their living room trying to decide on just the right name for our little Amy."

"That's why I brought it up, so we can now work on a name together tonight."

***

"Did you stop at the nursery window to see her, Frank?"

***

"Yes I did. In fact I was staring at her through the window, thinking how pretty she is and I was glad that you and her are alright."

"You know Frank, we have been blest with two beautiful daughters. Was she awake?"

***

"No, she was sleeping."

***

"Gee, the whole time I had her today she slept too. I even shook her gently but she kept right on sleeping."

Frank noticed the concern in his wife's tone and said, "Well, she was quiet when you were carrying her. You even said she didn't move much so maybe she's just going to be a quiet baby."

"Yes, that would be nice to have two good babies. Maybe later we could walk down to the nursery together. O.K., with you?"

"Sure, do you feel up to it?" Asked Frank.

***

"Yes, it would feel so good to get out of this bed." She answered.

***

"That's nice, but a bed is how and why you're in this bed right now!" He joked. Then with another kiss Frank asked. "How are you really feeling? Were you able to get some rest?"

"Well, I slept a little this afternoon, but I had a really strange dream. I am still shaken a bit from it."

***

"Oh really? What was it about?" He asked as he sat down on the side of her bed.

***

"If you wouldn't mind, I rather not talk about it right now. I know you asked but perhaps later. Let's work on a name for our little girl."

54

"Are you sure?" He questioned.

***

"Yes, I will tell you everything before you leave. But right now let's just work on a name for our new daughter and Amy's little sister."

Slowly she started to read aloud the names from the list, skipping and choosing at random but without any particular one capturing their attention.

"Gee Frank, I don't know, all these names but."

***

"Well now I was thinking that maybe we could pick a name that starts with an A, like Amy. What do you think?" Asked Frank.

"That's a good idea, I like that, Pumpkin! Then both our daughter's names would start with an A."

So she quickly turned back to the beginning of the A names. "Abigail...hmm...it means father's joy. What do you think Frank?"

"It's an old fashion name, I don't like it."

***

"O.K., we have Ada."

***

"No!" Frank said firmly and she second that.

***

"Adela, Adelaide, Adeline..." She glanced up at him and asked, "Adrienne?"

***

"No, it's a boring name." He answered.

***

"How about the name Agatha? Maybe she'll grow up to be another mystery writer." She joked.

With that remarked he made a face at her. So she continued on with Agnes, Aida and Aileen."Oh Frank, here's the French form of Amy, it's spelled Aimee, Alberta, Alethea, Alexandra, Alexis and here is one Frank, Alfreda!" At that Frank chuckled.

"I know let's name her after my mom, Alice. No on second thought better not. I wouldn't want to hurt your mom's feelings. Besides, I don't think Alice Gladys sounds that good together. Do you, honey?"

Frank just sat there with a funny look on his face and responded. "Keep going will you?"

***

"Sure, I have for your consideration the name of Alicia?" With no response she continued on with "Alienor, Aline, Alison and Alix. You know, Frank, not Alex but maybe Alison?"

"No, I don't care for it." He retorted.

***

"Alright how about Allegra. No I have it Frank! Alma!"

***

"Alma?" Frank repeated. "No, just no, be serious now and keep going."

***

"Do you think we are going to find a name tonight? All right, I know keep reading the names, Almera, Alta, Althea, Alvina, Amabel and Amanda. That is sort of nice. Don't you think?"

"Yes, we were thinking about that name for Amy, remember Di?"

***

"I do remember. Amanda was one of the names we had picked out together."

***

"Well Di, lets remember that one, perhaps we will come back to it, lets finish the rest of the names."

***

"O.K. Lets see the next one is Amelia, Amitty, Amy and here is her meaning, remember it means "Beloved". Gee Frank, I miss her, our little Amy. I can't wait to get home with her little sister."

***

"I know but you will be home in a couple of days. So enjoy the rest while you can. Now lets finish this, it's getting late and I am tired."

***

"Anastacia, no too long for a little girl. Andrea, Angela and the name does mean "Angel, Frank.""

***

With that Frank sat up straight and said, "Yes! I like that because first, her nickname would be Angie and it would end in IE and sound like Amy. Second, it's a pretty name and when you say it, Angela...has a bounce to it. Besides, you did mention that the name means "Angel".

"You really like this name, don't you Frank? Better than Amanda?"

"Yes. Don't you?"

***

"Amy and Angela, our daughters." She answered. But now what about her middle name? Amy Lynn and Angela what?"

Frank stood up and looked down at his wife and finished with "Beth". He then repeated her name. "Angela Beth."

She looked up at Frank and hummed "ABC", and with that answer they both chuckled together.

Frank than reached over and picked up the birth announcement certificate off of the nightstand next to his wife's bed and handed it over to her.

***

"Here you fill in our baby's name, because your handwriting is better than mine." He said handing her the pen.

Dianna very carefully printed each letter in the empty space that was meant for their daughter's name. She gave back the pen and form to her husband and once again Frank said, "Thank you for our new daughter and I love you."

"You don't have to thank me Frank, we made her together through our love. Isn't she beautiful?"

***

"She is definitely a beautiful little girl."

***

"Frank, she is so small and precious, our little Angela. You know what?"

***

"What?" He asked.

***

"Today when I was holding her and looking down on her little face, she reminded me of a little angel, laying asleep in my arms. You know what I did?"

" Go ahead, tell me."

***

"Well, first I unwrapped her blanket just to make sure she had ten little toes. I really checked our baby all over real well. She has such delicate hands and fingers. Do you know what I discovered about her ear lopes?"

"What's wrong with her ear lopes?" Inquired Frank.

***

"Nothing, honey, their fine. Angie's earlobes are shaped exactly like my younger sister's Nan. Nanny had pointed, pear shaped lopes. Oh Frank! My dream!"

He sat there quietly next to her on the bed and listened while she told him about the dream of her younger sister. When completely finished she asked. "What do you think it means Frank? It really frightened me!"

Shaking his head from side to side he responded. "I don't know what it could mean Di. It probably doesn't mean anything at all. It was just a bad dream you had. Nothing to really worry about, you always have strange dreams. He said as he gathered his young wife in his arms and held her close to his chest.

"I do hope that it was just a very strange dream Frank, for it seemed so real, especially Nan how she stood there in the midst so crystal clear. I felt as if she was trying to tell me something about our baby. Oh Frank, that dream really frightened me so! Almost as if Nanny herself had come back to me through Angie."

"Di, come on now, stop it, our baby is not your sister Nan!"

***

"But the dream Frank, it seemed so real to me."

***

"It was just a dream you had, just a dream."

SHARED EMOTIONS

"Was it a dream, Frank?" I asked aloud breaking the silence from within the truck.

**

"What did you say, Di?"

**

Dianna looked over at her husband and realized that she had spoken her thoughts out loud and quickly answered, "Oh nothing Frank, I was just thinking about something."

Frank didn't acknowledged his wife or looked her way, he just sat there rigid, with a blank like stare as he drove all of them closer to their destination. She watched him and secretly in her heart silently thanked God, reflecting upon his strength, dedication and love that had always been there for all of them. For this man was so young when married and responsibilities to take on such as being a husband and father. Later adding to all other duties in family life a disabled daughter. He could have thrown in the towel but chose to love, protect, provide and most of all be a husband and parent.

"I know you too must be deep in your own thoughts as I am now. You're bolding back tears Frank. Yes twelve years with tears of frustration and pain with Angie. Wasn't it just last night we laid in each other's arms and you opened up to me, and shared your inner most feelings? You told me that it would be so hard to give her up to someone else. That it was so unfair that we couldn't help our own daughter any more. It just felt like a win/lose situation. No matter which way you looked at it. How you wanted her home with us. But you knew in your own heart that we have tried and she hopefully will be better off where professional help will be provided. How it just hurts to know that you and I have done whatever we could for her. I guess the doctors were right, finally some day our little girl would have to get special help. So no matter what we do to try and make it better, we are all sad. Are you thinking what I am thinking? I failed her in some way? This should be our responsibility to care for her. Yes it is my responsibility, not strangers, but my responsibility!"

Since the day they were married or perhaps before than, the first time they were together, just two young teenagers who have clung together as one, an intercourse of love. Now an intercourse of conversation to deal with such an overwhelming decision. This act of judgment has now added to their heavy guilt feelings.

Dianna turned her head to glance back at the two girls. She noticed how Amy was rocking herself gently in the truck seat and still was looking out her side window. At that same moment, Amy reached for Angie's hand to pat it gently. With this soothing gesture from her sister, Angie ceased for a brief moment of her frantic whimpering.

Amy struggled hard to hold back her tears. She was immersed in her own personal thoughts and perhaps maybe unaware that touching her little sister's hand had created a sibling's comfort. Amy had once been so excited about the news of having a little sister. Someone to grow up with, a playmate, a soul mate, to share many of life's experiences together as they grew older. But instead twelve years of sickness and silence robbed of all her sibling's rights. She wanted always to be nothing more than a big sister and to know now that her right of being an older sibling would be very much different.

Dianna signed "O.K.?" to Angie and she responded back to her mother with a giggle. Only to look back out the rear window and see her things that were placed in the truck bed; Angie then resumed her soft whimper-like cry. The look in her eyes were spilt second mixtures of confusion, uncertainty, anger and fear. No words of signing could explain them away. So many emotions that the four of them had shared in that truck that morning. The four of them together but lost in their own thoughts. They were separate, different, but very much the same.

FEBRUARY 17, 1975

The morning after Angela's birth she was brought into the room for her morning feeding. Again the little one was sound asleep. The nurse informed her patient that the baby slept right through the night; further added that it would be nice if she continued to do so when she would go home.

"But we both know those two o'clock feedings are inevitable, right?" She kidded to Dianna. "Well, see how much of her formula you can get her to drink." She said as she handed over the bottle. "We tried earlier this morning, but the little sleepy-head just wouldn't stay awake long enough. She was slow at taking it, but do the best you can and I'll be back in a little while to check on you." The nurse said on her way out of the room.

"Alright now Angela Beth. Shall we try this again? Wake up and open your eyes for mommy." Dianna said while gently nudging the bottle nipple against her baby's lips.

She acted like one who refused to swallow the milk. The formula ran down from out of the sides of her mouth. There were no attempts from her to suckle. The baby's mother kept coaxing the nipple into her mouth and gently shook the bottle. Dianna tried to ignore that little voice within whispering to her. "This is not right. I don't think it's normal." Her baby just rested quiet and limp within her arms. She sat the bottle aside and grabbed a wet washcloth. Dianna wiped her little one's face and neck with it. While she cleansed the baby, the mother again noticed a bluish tint of the skin above the upper lip and the breathing seemed more labored, faster and shorter breaths than the day before. The eyelids upon the face appeared to be abnormal in size. In fact the whole left eye area looked smaller compared to the right.

"Dianna, stop it! You're looking for things that aren't there." She scolded herself. She tried to convince herself that what was being seen, felt and experienced in those past hours since the birth were not related to the past few months. "God, they must have checked her over real good. Surely the nurses and doctor would have noticed that something by now to confirm my fears. I did inform them that you weren't taking the bottle for me. Oh, I know they responded back to me. Well now Dianna, some new born babies are slower at first to grasp the skill of sucking."

She tried to convince herself that what was being seen, felt and experienced in those past hours since the birth were not related to the past few months.

But their casual matter-of-fact answers did nothing to calm her. If anything they made the young mother to feel like a nervous Nell, insecure and doubtful so she stopped the questioning. But just the same, she knew deep inside there was a definite difference there between her two girls after birth to take a bottle of formula. It was like day and night. Amy was so full of life and movement when she was held. So alert and wiggling. A wonderful feeling! But now there are no sounds of cries. The eyes, yes the eyes won't open to see how pretty they are. Yes, fears have grown stronger for this small infant. Anxiety swept through and fear closed around Dianna. She leaned back against the pillows and clutched her newborn daughter. "Please God, let my baby be alright!" She silently prayed with tears. Until the nurse returned, she sat there upon the bed rocking slowly back and forth. Dianna stared blankly out the window with Angela asleep in her mother's arms.

February 17, Visiting Hours

That same evening, Frank came to the hospital after work to spend some time with his wife. He had just finished having supper with Amy at his parent's home, and he brought a little message from their daughter to give to mommy.

"Amy says hi mommy, and she loves you and misses you and wants you and her sister to come home soon. Nana says that is what Amy talks about all day long. Nana and Papa both send their love." Remarked Frank.

"Oh, that is so sweet isn't it Frank? I know today when I talked with Amy, on the phone she sounded so excited and had lots of questions. I told her, mommy and her baby sister would be home in a couple of days."

The two of them then decided to walk down to the nursery and look in on their daughter. That night she was being held and rocked by one of the nurses sitting in the nursery's rocker. The nurse recognized the two and got up from the rocker. She walked towards the nursery window. About the same time two of their friends Jackie and Dean are walking down the hall toward them. But in Jackie's case it was more like waddling because she was due to deliver on the sixteenth. One could tell just by the expression on her face that she was anxious and very much uncomfortable. The nurse showed them Angela and their friends commented how small and pretty with all the black hair upon her head. The four of them stood at the window for a few minutes longer and made some small talk. Frank gave

Dean a cigar wrapped in a pink band. His friend took it and commented jokingly, "Thanks Frank, but next time you better try for a boy!"

"Ha! Ha! Will you two try again for a boy if this one's another girl?" Dianna retorted back to Dean.

"Not me. I am finished. Period. Girl or boy, no more!" Jackie exclaimed.

The four of them went back to Dianna's room and visited for a little while longer. Finally their friends left because Jackie was feeling tired and wanted to leave for home. Soon after Dianna's parents arrived and stayed for a short time. Her two older sisters, Sandi and Deb, along with their husbands also came that night to visit and see the new addition to the family. Frank gave his wife a kiss, said goodnight and left with them all because visiting hours were over. When everyone had left for home the nurse returned with Angela for her bedtime feeding. Again she nursed very slowly and laboriously from her bottle, taking very little of her formula.

FEBRUARY 18, 7:30 P.M.

Betty and her husband Harry had come for an evening visit. She wanted to give her congratulations to her brother Frank. When they arrived to the nursery floor the first stop was to be a glimpse at their new member of the family. But they were unable to see their new little niece when they arrived because there were too many people standing around the hallway outside the nursery, and the nursery window shades were closed. Toward the end of visiting hours Harry who becomes uncomfortable with hospital's surroundings, had suggested to his wife that they should consider about leaving, in order for them to have a chance to see the baby. Frank thanked them both for coming while Betty gave Dianna a hug and Harry shook Frank's hand before receiving a pink band cigar. But when the two of them walked back down the hall to the elevators, they had to pass the nursery window once again. The shades were still closed.

It was approximately 9:00 P.M., and outside Dianna's room she could hear the familiar sounds of the squeaking wheels on the carts that carried the babies to and from the nursery and their respective mothers. As usual some of the newborn infants were showing off their lung capacities with their crying. The sounds grew louder as the bassinet carts made their way down the hall toward Dianna's room. The squeaking noise stops in intervals of a few minutes, telling her that each mother is getting her baby.

Dianna sat up in her hospital bed propped up with a couple of pillows anxiously awaiting Angie's evening visit. She had utilized the time since the end of visiting hours by going to the bathroom, brushing her teeth, hair and had washed her hands. Now she was ready for an enjoyable visit with her daughter and wasn't going to allow those nagging doubts to interfere.

Reaching behind herself, she attempted to adjust the pillows by bringing one out to fluff and then replacing it. Once again, Dianna smoothed the bed covers by folding back the top sheet so it lain perfectly without a wrinkle. She pulled the sleeves of her nightgown down to cover her wrists and then folded her hands together on her lap and waited just staring at the door; her thumbs nervously crossing and uncrossing.

The sounds grew quieter out in the hall and soon they were no more, except for an occasional voice, and the rustle of a nurse's uniform as they passed Dianna's room. Minutes passed and she continued to sit in her bed anxiously waiting.

"Where is my baby? What's taking so long?" She asked herself. Dianna started to get out of the bed to look down the hallway, but stopped when she heard the rubber sole footsteps approaching her bedroom door.

"Yes! Here she comes now!" Dianna was surprised and startled at seeing the nurse entering her room without the baby. She walked over to her patient's bedside and reported kind of a matter-of-fact way that she wouldn't be getting her baby that evening. The little one was experiencing difficulty with breathing. Further the nurse stated that a call had already been placed earlier to Dr. Swynds.

Unable to move or speak, Dianna stared at her as the nurse continued to inform the patient that the doctor was still with her daughter. And then after a moment's hesitation, Dianna's nurse said, "Dianna, Dr. Swynds feels that for your daughter's best interest that she be transported to another hospital, not far from here.

"Why?" The only word Dianna was able to say.

***

"Because dear, they have an excellent new born facility. The baby will be transported by ambulance in an incubator. You can come out in the hall now and say goodbye to her before she leaves. Here, let me help you with your robe and slippers."

Dianna heard a small voice say, "Alright, but I still don't understand?" She stood there alone in the hallway of the maternity ward looking down into the incubator at her daughter. Little Angela was lying there within her confinement. She looked so pathetically vulnerable and for the first time noticeably ill, even to an untrained eye; for her color was tainted, her breathing sporadic and she laid there so very still.

Dianna wanted desperately to touch and hold her baby but she knew it was not allowed at that time. Unbearably she looked for someone, anyone to help her, for she felt so alone and helpless. There were many of activity going on all around her from the nurses caring for the infants to the mothers who were with their babies. "Someone please tell me this is not happening!" She cried out silently.

In the room to Dianna's left, a mother sat nursing her baby. Their eyes met in a look of knowing compassion. Both of the mothers that night were with their new baby, one healthy, one not. Within those few moments, other feelings of sympathy, thankfulness, envy and fear were transposed between the two women. Dianna turned her head away quickly. The little pink data card attached to the top of the incubator caught her attention.

***

Baby Girl, Angela Beth
D.O.B.: February 16, 1975
Weight: 6 lbs, 15 oz.
Length: 19"

***

"This isn't happening to you Angela. You are going to be all right! Please, dear God, hear me. Please allow my baby be all right!" I have to call Frank, I need him!"
"Good evening, Dianna."

***

She looked up and recognized Dr. Swynds who entered the ward through the double doors at the end of the corridor. He walked briskly down the hall toward Dianna, not saying anything further until he reached her side and there in the hallway for the next few minutes he explained to her what had happened to the baby. His tone was compassionate and cautious so as not to upset the mother further.

Angela had a seizure earlier that evening and had stopped breathing. The staff worked on her, a call was placed to Dr. Swynds and he returned to the hospital. Immediately upon the doctor's arrival, the staff had briefed of the infant's prior and current condition. After he had conducted a thorough examination and had carefully observed her responses, he placed a call to a team of specialists whose fields were new born babies with problems at birth. It was upon their advice that Dr. Swynds notified the hospital of the transfer of Baby Angela to their New Born Intensive Care Unit.

"Dianna, I have already called your husband and he is on his way here now. I am releasing you tonight from the hospital. I want you to go home. You, I think will be better off there instead of being here among the other mothers and babies."

Dianna didn't remember much more of what her doctor said that evening; nor could she think of anything to ask of him that regarded her baby's situation. For her whole being was overcome with the shock of realization, that all her fears and nightmares of the past months were no longer deniable. During the time the doctor was talking to Dianna, the hospital ambulance arrived and drove her little girl away. Everything was happening just too quickly!

Dr. Swynds left her to go back to the room, to get ready for the discharge. But first before she started packing, she needed to call someone. Without really thinking about who, she phoned no other than her mom. She needed to hear the familiar voice of comfort. For her parents wanted to come up immediately and be with their daughter. Dianna told her mother no because she was being sent home that night and there was nothing anyone could do right now. After speaking on the phone with her mother, Dianna's sister, Deb who was visiting with their parents that night, took the receiver to speak with her sister. After some questions of concern, she gave words of comfort and some advice. Dianna told her sister and her parents also that she would call back as soon as possible, when there was any more information about the baby's condition.

Frank walked in his wife's room as she was hanging up the phone. They held each other for a few minutes consoling one another; for there were no words that could still the fears and sorrow.

"After I take you home Di, I have to go to the other hospital and fill out some paper work for our baby. I don't know how long I will be. Do you think, that you will be all right at home? Do you want someone to stay with you?"

"Can I go with you Frank?" His wife pleaded.

***

"No Di. Dr. Swynds would like you to go home to bed and rest. A nurse is going to give you some medication before we leave here. Dr. Swynds wants you to take it to help calm yourself down."

Dianna did not further her plea, for she suddenly felt exhausted and drained. A nurse entered with the medication. A few minutes later an orderly had come in with a wheel chair. The orderly assisted her into the chair and then wheeled a benumbed silence. The only words spoken were "Thank You" to the orderly. Frank and Dianna did not speak during the short ride home to their apartment. When they arrived Dianna's sister Deb was there, for she had been so worried and concern for all of them, after her phone conversation came in about her new niece. Deb offered to stay while Frank left for the other hospital.

***

11:30 P.M.

Frank parked the car in the emergency lot and was directed to the hospital's newborn intensive care unit by the lot attendant. Once locating the unit, he let himself in through the double doors; and found himself standing in a wide hallway. To his right there was a large thick pane glass window and there he saw his little daughter hooked up to a heart monitor. A nurse was administering to the baby with what looked like to Frank a small baste with a rubber ball that she was squeezing something through a tube into his daughter's mouth, a few drops at a time.

He tapped on the window and got the nurse's attention. She motioned for him to enter into a small room next door where he could wash his hands and put on a sterile gown. Once washed and gowned she opened the door for him to enter into the room with her and the baby. In a very sympathetic and compassionate tone, the nurse briefed him of his little girl's condition since her arrival about 10:00 P.M. A heart murmur had been detected and she had stopped breathing twice but now was stabilized. Angela was gavage fed (force feeding through a tube) because she had a high-cleft condition (a congenital fissure in the roof of the mouth, which usually grows shut or surgically corrected).

Frank told his wife later, that it was like a bad dream, a nightmare watching his little daughter struggling with her new life. The hardest thing he ever had to face or do in his life. He sat there and how he had felt so helpless and so alone, as he watched the tube and monitored new born little daughter struggling for her existence. His mind wandered back three months earlier to a time when he and his friend Dean where in a bar talking about all the changes in their lives since high school days. Both being married at a young age, each already on their second child, occasional work layoffs they could both tolerate, but both agreed and hoped for healthy children because neither felt that they could handle a disabled child. Frank had also mentioned to his wife that he felt like he had been hit with a snowball as the cold reality struck him fully in the face.

Could it be, that what Dean and Frank had discussed just three short months ago was really happening? Is this a nightmare really coming true? All Dianna and Frank wanted to do was to wake up from this nightmare.

FALSE FRONTS

Baby Agela's report: Female
D.O.B.: 2-16-75
Time: 8:32 A.M.
Weight: 6 lbs. 15 oz.
Length: 19"
39 wks. gestation
Blood Type: AB Positive
Adm 2-18-75, time 10:36 P.M.
Admission Diagnosis: heart murmur, stopped breathing 2-19-75, normal infant electrocardiogram with physiologic degree of right ventricular predominance, sinus rhythm

***

February 19, the distinctive sounds of Nana's humming, dishes clattering and little Amy's chattering woke Dianna from a grogginess sleep. Frank's empty side of the bed told her that he probably had already left for work. Feeling so tired, from a restless night of tossing and turning; she felt not only exhausted and drained but also physically sore. So she lay there for a few minutes more absorbing the sounds coming from the kitchen. The all too familiar noises of domestic normalcy, that comforted her in order to place a few moments of sanity back into her morning and life.

Slowly she forced herself to get up out of bed. Standing there unsteadily, she felt a bit weak and dizzy but suddenly had the desire and need of a hot bath; for the front of her night gown was soaked with milk from her engorged breasts, giving off an unpleasant order. Besides a good soak might ease her bottom from the soreness and drawn feeling of the stitches.

Barefooted she walked out into the little hallway that separated the only bedroom from the bathroom. But before entering, Dianna stopped and stared towards the direction of her left at the empty white crib. It was lovingly placed, made up and stood against one wall in Amy's room; originally a breakfast nook off the kitchen, but now to be shared by the two little girls. Dianna's gaze wandered around the room decorated for little girls; with Amy's brass bed, her blue and white flowered coverlet with matching curtains, two small white dressers, the layette stocked dressing table, along with several assorted stuffed animals placed playfully on the two-tone pink striped carpet.

Again, her gaze reverted to the empty child's bed. Instead of an empty crib, but one that should be holding a sleeping and beautiful little baby girl. Dianna's eyes rested on the perfectly white baby's crib spread that was given as a gift to Angela by her Aunt Deb. Also spread across the crib's railing was a blanket with an unusual picturesque country scene in various hues of nature's colors, another precious baby gift by Frank's artistic cousin. Both treasured keepsakes would be packed away later, some day when no longer any use for them.

Dianna's attention from the girls' bedroom was broken by the sound of Nana's voice as she stood in the doorway of the two rooms. "Why good morning Di!" Her tone sounded light and happy even though she's probably dealing with her own sad, worried and questionable thoughts.

"Good morning mom. How long have you been here?"

**

"Oh, about a half an hour or so before Frank had to leave for work this morning."

**

"Did Frank get off alright?" Dianna inquired.

**

"Yes, he did and he seemed fine. Perhaps somewhat tired though from last night being at the hospital with Angela." Nana replied.

"Mommy!" Loudly shrieked Amy running toward her mother from the kitchen. She wrapped her small arms around Dianna's leg. Amy looked up at her mommy with a face full of love and smiles. Reaching down Dianna cupped her daughter's precious little face between the palms of her hands.

"Oh, I have missed you Amy! You been good for Nana?"

**

"Yes! Where's my baby sister?" She demanded.

**

How does one explain to a two and one-half year old child about something that even an adult just can't seem to comprehend or fathom? Dianna looked down into those big dark wondering eyes of the child. It should have been a happy and sharing time with the whole family together. Dianna was happy to be home, but there was someone missing; and something in that joyous moment about bringing a new baby home. The joy, warmth and happiness the family would share together was taken away from all of them.

Again Amy asked, "Where's my new baby sister, mommy?"

***

Amy's mom stammered for the right words and quickly mumbled something like, "Oh, your sister didn't come home with me. She is still at the hospital, because the doctors want to make sure she will be fine to bring home." Dianna really didn't know if her daughter understood what she was trying to say about Angela. For at the time her voice was shaky and straining just to keep from crying.

"I'll get your breakfast going, Di." Said Nana. "While you're in the tub."

***

"Thanks mom, for being here for Frank and Amy this morning." She reached over and gave her mother-in-law a hug.

"It's all right Di." Nana had taken off time from work to help keep her granddaughter during Dianna's hospital stay, but she was there now to care for all of them.

Little Amy satisfied for the time being with her mother's answers concerning her baby sister walked into the living room; and climbed up on the couch with one of her favorite stuffed animals to watch Sesame Street.

So while Amy was preoccupied and Nana was busy getting breakfast ready in the kitchen, Dianna took advantage of the time for a relaxing bath. Afterwards she made a phone call to the Newborn Intensive Care Unit. A nurse reported that Angela slept through the night and at that time was doing fine. Dianna asked if she could call again later to check on her daughter. The kind voice responded into the phone, "You can call at any time Dianna."

After talking and hanging up with the nurse on the phone, Dianna dialed her mom and told her about Angela's night and would keep her posted throughout the day. Her mother asked how everyone else was doing that morning? Dianna informed her that Frank had gone to work and Nana was with them at the house.

"All right honey, you keep your chin up, and if you need me let me know. Your Dad and I are here to help. I love you all."

***

After Dianna hung the phone back up she prayed secretly to herself to ask God for strength. For little did she know that she would have to be strong just like her mom once was. A mother of eight children, who had raised two disabled daughters and even lost one at a very young age. Dianna felt very fortunate that morning to have two caring and loving mothers and fathers as well. From her parents strength and love would help them through some very tough days ahead. The remaining of the day until her husband returned home from work Dianna rested and spent some much needed quality time with Amy. Then after supper Frank and Dianna together would go to the hospital to be with their new daughter.

***

The knowledge of Angela being in intensive care did nothing to prepare her or buffer the shock of seeing her baby for the first time in the mechanical and sterile surroundings that was now their daughter's only means of life support. Both Frank and Dianna seemed to be in a trance, *as they went through the motions of washing and gowning together in the* little room outside the intensive care nursery.

One of the nurses allowed them entrance into the nursery and pointed out the incubator in which their daughter laid, still tube and monitored. Husband and wife stood there in silence at the side of the small incubator holding each other's hand and just staring down. That was all both of them could remember together about that first visit when seeing their baby.

Frank and Dianna dealt silently with their own individual thoughts and feelings. Too painful to put into words as they anxiously watched their daughter struggle to stay alive. Not knowing whether she would live or die, the whole outcome of it all, added its exhausted toll upon them and staking a claim physically and mentally on their young lives. And in that emptiness guilt was planted, nourished and grew.

The only other memory Dianna had later of that first visit was before leaving that room, she stopped and turned around to look back at the incubator that Angela occupied. Dianna remembered thinking to herself that just one more glance at her baby. It might be her very last one, because Angela's life was uncertain and her time was questionable.

As they slowly walked through the parking lot toward their car, both of them were tensely quiet especially Frank. Every time his wife tried to say something, she would begin to cry, which only seemed to upset or anger him. Dianna couldn't wait to get into the car and go home, to lie down for her lower extremities were becoming more irritated and sore; and walking seemed to be adding to the growing discomfort. Frank opened the car door and helped his wife into the front seat. Once he was inside the vehicle, he had made a suggestion.

"Di, let's make a quick stop at River View Hospital and see Dean and Jackie's baby before going home."

"Why? I really don't want to go Frank."

***

"Well, I think we should, after all they did come up to see our baby." He retorted.

***

"Frank, I rather not tonight, I don't feel like it!"

***

"We don't have to stay long, just a few minutes." He insisted.

***

"Why can't you understand? That I am not feeling physically up to it, especially at this time because mentally I can't handle looking at other people's healthy babies right now." She angrily thought to herself. Dianna felt the tenseness between them and also knowing her husband's stubborn determination she agreed, just to keep the peace. For Dean was one of his childhood buddies, and she knew that her husband would not go alone.

"Alright Frank, just so we do not stay long."

***

Jackie, Dean and Frank stood together making small talk in the hallway. Dianna stood there too, staring through the nursery window at the newborns, an outsider looking in, isolated and bound by her own thoughts and feelings. Unwillingly and unable to share their joy or partake in the conversation without chocking on her own grievous tears. So she just stood there looking at one particular dark hair new born. Wishfully pretending that child was her own baby.

The next thirty minutes back in Jackie's room felt like an eternity. Sitting there on a hard plastic chair only added to the discomfort of the situation. For the most part Dianna was quiet. She did very little talking. When she did start to speak she would start crying. She desperately wanted to leave the room and go home.

For Dianna was in pain, physically and emotionally. And, with every passing minute getting more and more angrier and upset with Frank's seemingly unawareness for her feelings with especially when he inquired as to how Jackie was feeling. It just seemed to Dianna that he was more concerned about his friends instead of his own wife who was actually in pain also. Dianna remembered one comment to her by Jackie. It only added to her anger and hurt.

"Well, Dianna, you were able to have your baby on my due date and I had to wait three more days longer."

"Who really cares Jackie, about whose baby was born first? At least yours was born healthy." Dianna sarcastically thought.

When they finished their visit with Jackie and Dean, Frank and Dianna had to walk pass the nursery window again in order to exit. As she near the nursery the tears started to flow once more.

"Stop crying! Don't do it here!" Frank angrily admonished his wife loud enough for others to hear.

Embarrassed and hurt by his remark, she chocked back her sobs. That night at home Frank remained short tempered and moody with Dianna. Perhaps it was a reflection of his personal torment. He too had to pretend that he was happy for his friend about their baby girl, while he was going through his personal hell about another baby girl. Later on in their marriage, Frank unburdened his soul to his wife.

"I was very wrong. I should never have put you through that evening, it was wrong of me. I didn't realize it at the time, I was thinking only of our friends and not you. I am so sorry." Dianna also shared with husband how during that time as well, she was only thinking of her mental and physical pain.

Through the years as husband and wife, they both had to learn how to deal with and take charge of the situations that were to become their way of life.

BABY ANGELA: CHROMOSOME STUDIES

(Findings, Not Heredity)
February 20, 1975

Betty went over to her brother's duplex to invite her sister-in-law Dianna and her little niece Amy to spend the day with her and along with her two sons at the house. Nana was at work and Dianna's mom was caring for her three younger bothers and all of them felt that Dianna shouldn't be alone just yet. They thought it would probably be good for Amy to be occupied with her two cousins playing while her mommy could rest. The two women that day spent time together talking, watching the three children delighted to be in each other's company, praying within themselves and sharing thoughts and feelings about a daughter and niece that was not with them at that time.

Later that morning, Dianna called the hospital to get another report on Angela. By that time, late morning, the doctors should have completed their rounds. The nurse on the phone reported that her condition was still stable, basically the same, no new indications of seizures, still being monitored, tube fed and the doctors had ordered a chromosome work up. She explained to the baby's mother that this would help in order to determine information of the hereditary characteristics. Before hanging up the phone, Dianna thanked the woman on the other end and asked again if she could call back later in the day. With no hesitation and in a kind and sympathetic voice the response given to the caller was certainly please do, it's not a problem to answer any questions or concerns about your baby. Right after Dianna hung up the phone, she reported the news to Betty and than placed a call immediately to her mom. As always Dianna's mother said to hang in there, keep her strength and faith because only God would know what was best for Angela and the family; and before her mom hung up the receiver she sent her love to her daughter along whatever she could do for all of them. How wonderful it was to know the love, support and the concern coming from so many family members. This little family of four was gifted and knitted together with all their family's love and support, but most of all Dianna felt that faith and God's love was going to be the answer to all the prayers.

Frank had made a phone call to his sister's house on his lunch brake from work because he was concerned why his wife was not answering their phone at home. Betty explained to him that Dianna and Amy were spending the day with her. After talking to her brother for just a short time she then handed the phone over to Dianna. Frank listened intently about the recent news of his littlest daughter and later if possible a visit to the hospital. After the conversation with her husband, she was told he had to hang up and return to work. Before she heard the click from the other end, she also heard that familiar voice saying he loved her; and he would see them both later after work to take his family home.

Betty prepared lunch for all of them and insisted with concern for her sister-in-law to eat something. Dianna felt she had no appetite but Frank's sister explained to her how important it was so she could keep up the strength that was needed for her family. How her niece would need her mommy, Frank's dependence on his wife, her health as well so whatever was going to happen with Angela, strength was needed both for mentally and physically. During lunch Dianna talked Betty into driving her to the hospital so she could visit with Angela. Betty made arrangements with her husband Harry later to care for the children. He questioned about how long the time frame for their return home. Both women had no answer but to inform Frank if they were running late. Although Betty agreed to take Dianna, she was still very much concerned about Dianna's condition. But she caved in because of Dianna's shaken state to see her daughter. As a devoted mother herself she respected the other mother's wish. But Dianna didn't inform Betty how her lower parts were beginning to swell up and becoming more painful than the previous day. Dianna's only thought was the need to see her baby because phone calls just weren't enough. She could not let herself rest until that visit to the hospital to see and be with her little one. Betty agreed to drive after listening but still was hesitate only because she felt and said that rest and off the feet was important. Dianna made a promise to do only and after her mission was completed. That promise would be fulfilled but how of a painful promise later!

***

Immediate family only was allowed to be in the nursery of ICU, Betty stood outside watching through the partition window. Washed and gowned up, Dianna entered the unit alone to stand by her daughter's incubator. As usual she was asleep. Angela looked so peaceful even with all the monitoring leads attached to her little body.

Tears swelled up in the young mother's eyes and Dianna choked back a sob as she looked at her baby in the incubator. So tiny and defenseless looking, that mom's heart ached for her little one. Dianna stood still and silent but within her heart she prayed aloud to God, that her precious child wasn't suffering. That she would sleep through this bad time, this nightmare and she would wake up well and healthy from this, the whole family's inescapable dream.

One of the ICU nurses walked over to speak some reassuring words about Angela's morning. There were no changes from what had been told earlier. The nurse informed Dianna that she could open the little portholes to the incubator and put her hand in to touch her little girl. Perhaps the older woman noticed how tired and shaky the infant's mother was, for she brought over a chair and insisted that the younger woman should sit down. Reaching through both portholes Dianna was able to touch her precious baby's foot with one hand and enclosed her little hand with the right hand. It was warm inside and mom let her hands linger there for some time. Whispering in a choked and whimpering voice, "Mommy is here Angela. Mommy is here."

Dianna looked up and over at Betty who stood at the other side of the window. For Angela's aunt stood alone, feeling helpless to both mother and child and graciously moved by the scene before her eyes through the glass partition. Betty smiled back through her tears. Some time later, she confided in her sister-in-law, how hard it had been for her to watch as Dianna's hands reached through the little doors of the incubator and touched her little niece. Betty said to her sisterly friend, "The hardest thing I went through emotionally."

Dianna didn't want to leave Angela, her little baby girl, alone with these strangers who would take over the necessary care, but these strangers or hospital nurses had the knowledge and skill to perform their duties. Soon Dianna would come to know, understand, depend and respect toward the caring and loving staff that would be part of her baby's life. But now she knew it wasn't right or thoughtful to keep Betty waiting so long. Time was passing into very late afternoon and Betty needed to get back to her family. Dianna knew as well to return to her other daughter who was waiting for her mommy. Besides the pain she was experiencing so badly below in her vaginal area caused her though to strongly hesitate the thought to move, stand or even the notion to walk. For if possible Dianna really didn't want Betty to know how much discomfort that she was experiencing. Slowly Angela's mommy removed her hands from within the incubator and grabbed the arms of the chair and stood up on legs that were shaky and rubbery feeling. One more time she looked down into the incubator at her tiny infant and said in tones of love and assurance that mommy would come back very soon. With her head down and bowed in prayer she prayed. "Oh God, please, I beg you to watch over my baby. So I can bring her home healthy, to care for her and that her daddy and older sister Amy can be with her also. Please God, I want my baby home with her family, and with all of her family."

Dianna turned slowly away from the incubator and awkwardly walked toward the doorway that lead to the other room where Betty was still standing at the window like a guard or guardian angel. Without any words but with strength, awareness of much mental and physical pain, love and friendship she watched Dianna removed and discarded the hospital's gown and grabbed her coat and purse. Together they exit the unit quietly and tearfully for fear they both would cry aloud if either one had spoken a single word. They proceeded dilatorily toward the elevators where Dianna collapsed unexpectedly against Betty. The picture of one woman helping another one, who was apologizing, emotionally crying and laughing while being backed up and propped up against the wall railing had to be priceless. Dianna leaned against the railing while Betty fled rapidly to find a wheel chair. Upon Betty's returned with the chair she hoped and prayed that she would find Dianna still against the wall and not on the floor. Once the invalid was sorely seated in the chair the two of them laughed about the incident. Perhaps this time was given as a time to release some pressure of the eventful afternoon. The collapsing had caught both of them off guard and Betty was very concerned and worried about Dianna's welfare. She insisted that a visit should be promptly to Doctor Swynds office before returning home.

✱✱✱

Dr. Swynds was very shocked and surprised to see his unexpected patient arrived in his office and upon his examination when he discovered that Dianna was extremely swollen and irritated within her lower regions. He sympathetically explained that Angela needed to be in the hospital. There were complications to her birth that needed medical attention that only specialists could provide answers for her problems. He no longer gave any signs of being agitated with his patient. For the doctor that Dianna confided in about her pregnancies, he mayhap understood the worries and concerns of his patient going to check on her new infant. He knew that she was a good mother and she would have to be a strong mother for this new arrival in their family. So he told Betty to take her sister home and put her straight to bed with ice packs. Also he wanted Betty to inform her husband Frank of her highly emotional and physical state. The last four years the good doctor treated his patients, Frank and Dianna, before they were even married. Frank insisted upon that his pregnant girlfriend, soon to be his wife, should be seen by his family's doctor. But he always connected Betty and Dianna as sisters and not Betty and Frank as siblings. A future cherished thought for the good doctor.

✻✻✻

For the next three days, Dianna was in the care of her brother's wife, Judy, who upon hearing about her brother's sister condition came over and packed Amy and her sister-in-law up and moved mother and daughter to her home where she could care for both. Dianna didn't feel that it was necessary but Judy insisted. It was good for little Amy to spend time and play with her three cousins. During those three days, Frank kept busy running from work to our apartment, the hospital to check on Angela and over to his brother-in-law's house to visit the rest of his family. Dianna continued to keep in touch with daily phone calls not only to the newborn care unit and staff at the hospital, but also the three specialists in charge of her baby and phones calls to family members as well. For both Frank's and Dianna's families were very much concerned and supportive to the young couple and their newly arrival. Everyone also include thoughts and love for little Amy as well. Prayers, love and hope were always sent or called for best wishes for the family. It was truly a time when family rallied together and turned to God for trust and guidance.

✻✻✻

Baby Angela:
2-21-75: cleft x-ray, difficulty with sucking, fed on and off tube feeding by method of gavage
2-24-75: mother held baby first time and bottled fed, one ounce

The short stay with the family gave Dianna the opportunity to spend some quality time with her family. John and Judy's three children helped Amy by passing the days with play and much mischief. Dianna herself was feeling more rested, and the swelling and tenderness had lessened up some to make movement and walking much more tolerable. Several days later feeling physically better, Frank and Dianna went back to the hospital together to visit their daughter. One of the ICU nurses was kind enough to place a rocking chair for Dianna to sit in at the side of her baby's incubator. Then she gently lifted the little one out of the incubator and placed the sleeping infant in the arms of her mother with the monitor leads still attached to the baby.

So many emotions flooded through Dianna as she sat there with Frank at her side, holding their precious gift and weeping silently. Some reason she seemed unsure and afraid at first but then elated to be finally able at least to have the mother's love, a special contact with her baby again. She so much wanted and needed to give that love, a gentle warm touch, a voice of flowing words to let her baby know and hear that mommy and daddy was there; a slow motion of rocking to reinforce the feeling of natural love between mother and child. Dianna casually allowed her eyes to peer upon the young man seated by her side. She noticed he sat hunched forward in the chair with his elbows resting on his thighs and his chin placed on both of his crisscrossed fingers. He stared down at his tiny daughter and said for only mom's ears to hear, "She is so beautiful, just like Amy, but only smaller. Are you happy Di, now that you can hold her?" He than looked up at his wife with eyes of love but tinted with tears. With another set of tinted eyes he heard a soft, yes.

One of the unit's nurse asked Dianna if she would like to try and bottle feed the baby while she sat there. Angela was able to take one ounce of her formula with quite some effort on her part. The struggle itself to consume just that one small ounce of formula left her quite exhausted and she continued to sleep in her mother's arms. Dianna asked her husband if he wanted to hold his daughter, but he replied no; perhaps his hesitation was also pain, fear or even a little uncomfortable about moving the baby at that tender moment. Instead Frank clasped her little hand in his. Dianna couldn't imagine what was going through his mind at that time or how he must have felt as he sat there by her side. Both mother and father were having much difficulty with their own individual feelings, trying to digest and cope with the situation of their little daughter.

Just to touch her and to feel that little body against Dianna, her listless vulnerability was creating a strong resolution on the mother's part to care, protect her from any pain and to simply love Angela no matter what the future's outcome. The infant's father had already felt that since the first night he saw his baby girl in the newborn ICU unit.

Three days later Baby Angela had progressed enough that she was moved from the ICU and placed out on the unit floor. The family was then able to take her home sometime around the end of February. Upon her release a nurse informed the parents to be aware of possible seizures, if she had any problems with taking the bottle to spoon feed her, her formula and any questions or concerns to call the specialists. Also, a follow-up appointment was to be scheduled within the week.

For Frank and Dianna it was a very anxious and nervous homecoming with their second born, for they were totally unprepared, uninformed, inexperienced and very young; and little did they realize that for the next twelve years, they were to become child advocates not only for Angela's rights but for their own survival as a family unit in a social system that seemed oblivious to special needs. Even Amy so excited at finally seeing her baby sister would all too soon have to deal with all the changes that were soon to affect her life as well. To deal with too many different or unusual incidents and situations that would place a heavy burden and responsibilities on the whole family. Right down from small to large decisions that could deter the outcome of a destination this family would travel. They would have to travel on an uneven road certain with unsightly curves and rapid stops to make along the way. To travel even on this questionable road of life, the inevitable decision twelve years later could possibly do to this family? Could this only be just a beginning to an ending of twelve anguished filled years? But always this road must be travel on with hopes and dreams, pain and fear, prayer and trust. Always this road traveled with swift curves, unexpected, unwanted and some appreciative stops along the way.

PART TWO

ANGIE'S SECOND HOME

Dianna had always half-jokingly referred to the nearby medical center as Angela's second home or home away from home, because for the first three to five years of her life, she was continually in and out of the hospital. Angela's mom would tell everyone that they were responsible for the building of the new and improve parking facilities. Her daughter's numberless admissions were usually due to an emergency situation.

April 11, 1975 admittance: pneumonia, undeveloped left pupil, possibility of seizure activity, apnea spells, turns blue, close to death, dusky color, cyanotic during feeding, difficulty swallowing, when feet pinched does not cry

On this date was Angela's first bouts with and one of numerous attacks of pneumonia. Just prior to this first hospital admission Dianna had already taken her daughter to one of the specialists for a check up, Angela had developed a cold.

This was the very first seizure Angela had that occurred during this time. Dianna phoned her mother if she could possibly come over to care and spend some time with her granddaughter. She explained how nice it would be to take Amy out shopping for both girls Easter outfits, and how important to spend a little quality time with her oldest daughter. But when mother and daughter's enjoyable outing came to an end, their return home of fun was stopped abruptly when Dianna found her mother along with Frank's mom, hovering over Angela in the makeshift room where the girls slept. Immediately Dianna sensed that there was something wrong and deposited her purchased articles onto Amy's bed. Her mother quickly informed the daughter that Angela had stopped breathing and that her lips had turned dark blue. Dianna's mom had never witness someone having a seizure and her first thought was to call Frank's mom for help and support. She lived only a block down the street and made it over to the house in just a short of two minutes.

By the time Nana arrived, the baby was no better. The little one's eyes had rolled back, her arms and legs were rigid and her coloring was even more cyanotic. Nana made a suggestion for them to call the rescue squad. Both grandmothers agreed that their granddaughter needed some air or oxygen to assist her breathing. By the time the paramedics arrived and they examine Angela, she was beginning to regain normal condition from the seizure. The two men had given instructions to Dianna's mother that her daughter should call the baby's doctor immediately upon her arrival home.

Naturally, both grandmothers were shaken from the frightening experience shared together with their granddaughter. But the two older women put on a brave front, in order not to distress the mental and emotional environment of the rest of the family. Dianna's mother assured her daughter by giving her a gentle hug and saying, "It's alright now honey, they cared for her." Nana's act of boldness also gave the older granddaughter confidence that her little sister would be all right. The grandmothers were there together, giving support to each other, concerned for their little granddaughter and trying to console each other, both grandchildren and their daughter. Dianna realized how fortunate she was to have two strong mothers in her life. Much gratitude of thanks to God for the love, support, the unselfish giving of themselves that day and the special gift of mothers that He created to ensure an everlasting family bond.

Angela's family now realized that these were the signs of an apnea seizure, until Dianna had called the doctor. He advised the mother to take her daughter immediately to the emergency room.

The hospital staff examined the young infant and informed the baby's specialist who then recommended that she should be admitted. For this too would soon be the pattern for the family to follow with Angela's numerous admissions.

***

Throughout all this young infant's life with her early hospital endurance, Dianna whenever she would leave the facility, the uneasy feelings of helplessness and sensation of fear that she probably would never see her precious baby alive again. If at all possible before Dianna would have to leave her baby's bedside because of her job or other family obligations, Dianna would hold her little daughter, calmly reassuringly with words, gentle touches and along with a tender kiss placed upon the soft, sweet smelling head of her baby. After that the young baby's mother would exit the infants unit into the hallway standing outside the large room looking in through the glass window at the hospital bed that confined, held and separated infant and mother. The baby's mother would stand alone peering in through the glass partition crying softly, hoping and praying the guardian angel and God would keep vigil over her little one, that God would heal the physical aspects of her life so her daughter could return home one day very soon with the family. Sometimes when Angela's parents visiting together, they would stand outside the window feeling so damn helpless and afraid. Frank would urge his wife to leave and then put his arm around Dianna's shoulder and tried to make a confident statement such as, "Come on Di, it's time for us to go home to Amy now. Let her get some rest for a little while. Our little girl will be just fine. You know she is getting the best care."

Frank's declaration of words to his wife was true and it gave them both some comfort, because the hospital personnel were always so caring, understanding and patient with their daughter. Sometimes Dianna would send to the infant unit's care givers, lab technicians and the doctors a "Thank You" card expressing the family's gratitude for the special ways of showing and giving tender loving care to Angela.

One of the specialist doctors on several occasions told Dianna what an excellent job she and her husband were doing with their daughter. Sometimes he would pat the baby's mom on the shoulder and say, "You're doing a great job mom." His acknowledgements always boosted the mother's spirits.

***

It was during one particular hospital stay, only after the baby's condition had stabilized, that Dianna had requested to have a doctor examine her daughter's left eye. Since the birth of her child, the mother seemed to detect she thought at times a size abnormality between both of the eyes. Dianna had repeatedly brought up her concerns to husband's attention, but he himself had not noticed any size variation and would just pass it off as an over reaction on his wife's part. But an examination by one of the hospital's optometrist did confirm that their daughter's left pupil never totally developed. The pupil was in a shaped as a tear dropped. The parents were able to bring their baby girl home on the twenty-eighth day of April.

The young parents had come to realize that their daughter would require constant care around the clock. Also the family life style changed drastically from normal every day living to a very stressful, unsure and anxious way of life. At one time the family consisted of three. They were happy with many good moments shared together as a family. The freedom to do and perhaps even go whenever possible. Perhaps even a promising future for the family, with many thoughts of hopes and dreams to look forward. Although the family was still happy but fearful, there would still be good moments only fewer ones, the air was taken out of their freedom like a balloon deflated and the future would only hold plenty of uncertainties, hopeful thoughts, and wishful dreams for a unsure existence or future that the three of them had all too soon learned and tried adjusting to. It was a beginning for the family to cherish, respect life, be happy and thankful for the good moments and the special gifts that God bestowed upon them, take one day at a time and never try to take life for granted.

***

Because Angela was so quiet and she never cried or made any noises that babies usually make for wanting to be fed or changed; Dianna had to be always on guard watching her closely during the day and at bedtime. At night the parents would take turns getting up several times to make sure she was alright. This left the father tired to get up for the following work morning and throughout the day on the job, leaving him to be exhausted at the end of the day. The mother was also tired in the morning when trying to awake her husband. Less sleep caused her not to give enough quality time with Amy, her oldest, tired during the long and tedious care for Amy's little sister and small things went undone in order for the more important things to be accomplished first.

The baby's feedings were long and tedious because of being spoon fed since she had very little sucking ability and difficulty with swallowing the formula. Sometimes while Dianna was feeding the infant, Amy would stand at her mother's side just observing and being very inquisitive about Angela. Questions as to why mommy was using a spoon to put some milk into the baby's mouth. Why her little sister was not using a baby bottle like her baby dolls. For her mommy sometimes played babies with her and showed how important to care for the baby. Amy being so young still noticed that mommy was not feeding her sister with the bottle. It was very hard to find words, to explain to her oldest that little sister was different about taking her milk, so the small young mind could understand.

Frank and Dianna always tried to answer their oldest daughter's questions thoroughly and patiently. So that way Amy would understand about her sister's health condition, explanations of certain life changes, why mommy and daddy would be extra tired but with out using it as a constant excuse and at all costs to show love, devotion, care and affection to both daughters. And from this sharing, Amy grew not only to understand by literally and action form, but to become Angela's loving, big sister and her protector. So from early on a touch of normalcy planted and watered by the parents helped for the function of family life growth.

TWO DAYS LATER

April 30, 1975 hospital admittance: convulsions

A convulsion is a fit, or seizure, caused by abnormal activity in nerves in the brain. Convulsions occur more often in children than in adults, because a child's developing brain is more sensitive to disturbances rather than that of a fully, grown brain of an adult.

The causes of convulsions in children may vary, but in Angela's case, she seemed to fit in every cause and pattern of having convulsions. In most cases the cause is either unknown or related to a very high fever caused by a minor infection. However, convulsions may also occur in children with brain damage or having a brain tumor as in the case of Angela, both of these reasons applying. On May 12, 1975, after twelve days in the hospital, the parents once again took their daughter home.

SEVENTEEN DAYS LATER

May 29, 1975, admittance: difficulty with her breathing, vomiting described as projectile, about two feet, high pitched crowing sound while crying, (father's description of cry as emotionless, hollow, empty, like nothing behind it), additional hospital tests that were ordered on infant resulted in findings of congenital malformation of the larynx, retrorse goiter, vascular abnormalities producing constriction, thick uvula, head: normal cephalic, eyes: strabismus and coloboma of left iris (a condition in which the eyes can not be simultaneously focused on the same spot, when one or both eyes turn inward)

Prior to the admittance on May 29, just after feeding Angela at home, the baby was laying in her mother's arms. Dianna remembered that her face took on a strange look. Around her daughter's mouth was very blue and all of a sudden the baby vomited and it went nearly halfway across the living room.

Amy saw what her sister had done and it frightened her so she began to cry. Dianna asked Amy if she could do mommy a big favor and be a big girl. Mommy told her oldest that she needed some help and if Amy could get a cloth diaper from the baby's table in their bedroom. Amy happily ran off and quickly returned with not only one diaper but with several of them in her small hands. She also returned with lots of questions. Mom was very unsettled by the incident of what took place with her infant. Dianna tried very hard to keep Amy also at ease while the cleaning and caring was going on for her sister.

Later a phone call was made to the specialist to explain what took place during feeding time. Once again he suggested a visit to the emergency room for a check up for the baby. Again the ER staff reported back to the doctor and another admission was required.

The parents again were able to take their baby girl home from a short stay at the hospital on June 2, 1975. This was the third admission at the medical center.

CHRISTMAS

December 5, 1975, hospital admittance: bronchitis

December 9, 1975, hospital admittance: pneumonia, further testing, skeletal development that of a six month old, infant does not sit alone or put pressure on feet to stand, scoots on back, stares at ceiling even with position change, has staring episodes, hospital records states that mother is nervous and depressed

✳✳✳

The month of December, of 1975, Frank and Dianna's daughter, Angela was diagnosed as mentally retarded. It was very hard for the parents to believe or to accept that their little girl could possibly be called retarded. Yes it was true that Angela was born with some problems, the parents knew that her health was jeopardized with issues to prevent her from growing in normal stages. But they thought it was way too soon to put a label such as mentally retarded.

There were times such as near her hospital bedside or in the children's play room when professionals such as the intern students, along with the doctors, some being specialists and nurses would observed Angela scooting on her back while tilting her head backwards in order to see where she was going. She used her feet to push herself across the floor.

Mom recalled one particular day when she and her baby girl left the room to escape the other infants, toddlers and their parents. Dianna carried her child lovingly in her arms for a walk down the hallway. Together mother and daughter would stop at various places throughout the hall, looking at some paintings of different pictures from fairy tales or stories of characters to decorate the children's unit. Each piece of colorful art was there to brighten the daily lives of so many toddlers and older children that were admitted because of various medical reasons.

Dianna would stop and try to have Angela look also at the brightly colorful images drawn and painted on the walls and windows. She tenderly held her daughter as she explained in expressive words, sometimes in a shaky voice, but bravely or supportive in hopes to make her little one feel secured and loved. Even to stop and stare out the hospital hall window to look at the cold, bare, desolate and lonely view. To see the trees bare from the coverage, the sky looking gray with heavy snow clouds and the cold wintering atmosphere scene surrounding the hospital.

Again mother hopefully would talk in a soothing tone to her daughter about going home and all being a family. How Amy her big sister missed having a little baby sister around, especially at night when the two of them could share being in the same room together. How daddy would come home from work and not have all three of his girls waiting at home for him. How their home took on the coming holiday with the Christmas tree and decorations, awaiting the arrival of Angela to come home and enjoy the many colored lights with her big sister. Just like the family waiting in the celebration of the birth of baby Jesus. The most important gift that mommy and daddy wanted was to have all their family together.

To end the melancholy spirits of sadness and despair, Dianna moved away from the window and continued to walk down the hallway toward the playroom with her little girl. She stopped and looked through the small viewing window and saw that the room was opened for the children. On impulse she quickly decided to enter in hopes to lift her spirits and spend some playtime with Angela.

Mom swiftly glanced around at the few children that were in the room along with a nurse stationed in the area. She smiled at the little ones playing with various toys that were provided for them. Two small children sat at a child's table that contained baskets or plastic containers filled with crayons, paper, magic markers and other craft materials.

Dianna spotted a place away from the children where she could gently put Angela on the floor for her to lay or scoot around. There was nothing there in the room for her baby to sit in that would be safe, for Angela was unable to sit up alone. Once she had her daughter down, mom looked for a few things perhaps Angela would be interested in playing with, or looking at or inspire her baby to move about freely.

For a while mother played and talked with her little girl. She tried to get her daughter to grab for a toy with her hands. But Angela would only lay there on the floor as if she was bored with her surroundings. At one point she moved by scooting across the floor on her back and tilting her head backwards. A small child noticed how Angela was moving and came near and asked Dianna questions. "What was wrong with her? Why was her hair that way? Why was she moving that way?" After all children are innocent and curious. It did not embarrassed or unsettled mom to answer the inquiry child. Dianna started to give a reply back when the nurse came over and directed the youngster to go play and not bother the baby's mother.

To answer a child's simple question would have been so much easier than to endure the looks or stares of interns and doctors. This was the very day when several of them would come in and pointed out Angela in the room. They stood there in the room with notepads and pens in hands and observed the baby's way of maneuvering herself about on the playroom floor. The house doctor or doctors gave medical information to the students or interns in regards to Angela's health condition. Sometimes a few of them would stop writing in order to ask a question. Answering only in hushed or mumbled voices and in medical terms that were unrecognizable or understandable for the unintelligible people with out having the medical knowledge or garble.

Make things even worse when these highly educated people do not take the time to notice or acknowledge that the mother is in the same room on the floor next to her child. Not even to inquire how mother and daughter were doing that day or for that matter what they were doing together on the floor. To take a few moments from their busy schedule to allow a parent ask if they have any questions or concerns regarding their child. Or simply explain in lament terms what or why they are all standing around staring, gawking writing and talking about the patient. Interns and doctors do not always know how it feels to have your child on display like a specimen or treated like some kind of guinea pig, when they themselves can't find answers or understand the health issues that effect others.

The only way possible the professionals of the medical field would know how a parent felt, they themselves would have to experience the same ordeal in life. To live it, is the answer or take classes from those who do live it.

The parents are responsible for raising and nurturing an individual who needs special care on a daily basis. It's important for parents to be recognized for their work and complemented when doing a job in life that requires so much time, effort and love that is given to their children. It is hard enough performing the job as a good parent with normal children, even harder on special ones. Angela's specialists always gave the parents, support, time, recognition and compliments in ways of a pat on a shoulder or in kind words for the great task of caring for their daughter.

As infants sitting in an infant seat or swings, sometimes mothers have to place a small diaper or blanket along side of the baby or in front to prop or give support. This way mothers can take the baby from room to room and do various chores around the house, never leaving baby alone but mother can still accomplish some things during the daytime.

Whenever mom placed her baby into the infant seat and also after securing or snapping the safety belt together, she would always have to put several cloth diapers along the side of her daughter to give support. Mom would try to position her baby's head so daughter could look from side to side. But Angela would just simply stare never really focusing on anything in particular, never moving her head to follow her mother's movements in the room and sometimes her little head would fall back in a slant never blinking her eyes, just staring upwards.

She was always so very quiet, never making any noises of any kind. No crying, no sounds of squealing, not any signs of feelings, no moving of her small hands or feet. Just still and limp like a rag doll. Nothing even when mother tried to talk or play with her daughter. Even when her big sister Amy would be present within the room chattering away, playing or being right near her little sister.

***

Easter of 1976 Frank and Dianna were blest to have their daughters together to celebrate as a family. The two girls sat together on the sofa, side by side, wearing the same identical outfits. Amy was wearing a green and white checker skirt and top, white anklets with lace trimming the tops and little white paten leather strapped shoes. The child's very light brown hair in ringlets with small white-bow hair clips. She was sitting next to her sister holding her hand with a big smile upon her adoring doll like face.

Angela was propped up with small blankets in her infant seat. She was leaning over slightly to one side away from Amy with her head tilted up wards and just staring up towards the ceiling. Angela was wearing an identical outfit except for hers was pink and white checkered. Upon her feet were small white and lacey socks and little white shoes. Her half-shaven head of dark hair showed her numerous intravenous marks from all of her hospital stays. Even the bottoms of her little feet were scarred from all the IVs; and even today you can still see the scar marks at the bottoms of her feet. But her angel like face was marred with a sickly appearance. To daddy and mommy, these two little girls were the most precious angels that God had given to them.

***

Christmas Eve, 1975, ten months old

Angela's first Christmas with her family followed the family tradition. The four of them would make the holiday rounds to both parent's homes that evening. Starting first with Nana and Papa's house. All gathered there were Frank's sister Betty, her husband Harry and their two sons, Harry jr. and Brad.

Mom had dressed both girls in red and white velvet dresses. Amy's hair in ringlets pulled back with red and white berets completed her festive outfit. But Angela's hair still too short and uneven from her numerous head shavings would not even hold a small barrette. Her scalp still tender and scarred.

That evening when Aunt Betty and Uncle Harry arrived at Nana and Papa's house, they both stopped, looked and remarked what a beautiful and precious picture the two sisters made sitting together on Nana's sofa in the dining room. Uncle Harry left the room and returned with his camera to take the lovely Christmas picture.

Later that evening after the family had eaten their Christmas Eve meal, Angela started experiencing some respiratory distress. So mom sat down on one of Nana's dining room chairs with her legs extended outward, knees locked and placed her daughter face down on her legs, her head toward mom's feet. Cupping her hands, mom pounded gently on her daughter's back and shoulders for the next several minutes while the family watched on in concern.

This procedure known as "postural drainage percussion" was taught to the parents by the hospital staff to use to help loosen the phloem in her throat, chest and alleviate the congestion within her lungs. For the next hour, Dianna faithfully executed the procedure or intervals every fifteen minutes but to no avail. Her condition seemed to be worsening with every passing moment, causing anxiety to everyone and making the family feel uncomfortable.

So Frank and Dianna decided for the well being of their daughter and the family's best interest to go home earlier, leaving their exchange and wrapped gifts for later. There at home the parents could better administer to their little one. Once at home, dad set up the vaporizer and got his daughter's medications ready for mom while she continued the pounding procedure upon Angela's back.

It took some time getting Angela comfortable and settled for bed that evening. After the parents had finished with the immediate and necessary administrations for their daughter, Dianna phoned her parents to inform that the four of them were unable to come over and join the family for Christmas Eve. Her mother was very sympathetic and understood the reason for them not to join the others. Dianna's mom sent her love to all of them and told her to take good care of the little one and also not to worry about canceling Christmas Eve at her house. She asked how Amy and Frank were doing? Dianna mentioned that daddy was keeping Amy occupied with a story. After hanging up with her mother, she than placed another call to Frank's parents to let them know that Angela was doing a little better and was put to bed for the evening, but they would have to keep a very close watch on her throughout the night.

Frank and Dianna ended what was left of their Christmas Eve by spending some quality time with their other daughter Amy. They put on some Christmas music, turned the tree lights on for her and the three of them ate a cookie along with some milk.

Almost three years old Amy was somewhat disappointed and confused with the outcome of the evening. Mommy and daddy tried to explain that her little sister needed to go home because she was not feeling well. They could not give the proper care for her at Nana and Papa's house. But not for her to worry because her little sister would get some rest in hopes to make her feel better by morning.

Also on Christmas day her and daddy could go over to Nana's to pick up their gifts. Even grandma and grandpa would visit the next day to bring their gifts as well and they could all visit together and exchange their special things. Before putting Amy to bed that night, mom and dad let Amy open up one small gift that was from them and helped her to prepare a plate of Christmas cookies and a glass of milk for Santa.

Then Amy kissed her daddy goodnight and in return he told her how much that he loved his big girl. Why she should go directly to sleep so Santa could make his stop at their house. Mommy took her daughter's small hand and led her to the room where she and her sister shared together. Amy climbed up onto her bed and laid her head down on the pillow.

Mommy pulled the blankets up around her, gently touched her precious daughter's cheek and bent down to place a tender kiss upon her child's forehead. Mom said goodnight and as she moved away from the bed, mom said in a quiet voice, "I love you, Amy."

She than tip toe softly over to Angela's crib and peered down onto the sleeping infant. Her little one was breathing better and she seemed to be resting more comfortably. Again in her quiet voice mom whispered to her baby, "I love you, Angela. God, please keep my baby girl safe through the night and watch over both of my daughters. Amen." With that she left their room and headed back into the living room to spend some much needed time with her husband.

***

December 31, 1975 - January 10, 1976 hospital admittance: pneumonia and seizures.

Angela's bronchitis attacks would usually develop into a high fever and pneumonia. No matter what precautions the parents would take, and always resulted in a hospital stay. So for the first three years of Angela's life, her parents were afraid to go anywhere especially in the winter time; and because of this, mom felt robbed of Angela's early childhood, because of all her illnesses and hospitalizations. All of the "everyday and normal" things during a child's first years, her mother completely missed out on. Frank and Dianna felt cheated and wondered if their youngest daughter would even survive.

Not only did mom miss out with Angela, but also she felt that time was taken away even with her oldest daughter, Amy. Because of the constant twenty-four hour care that mom had to devote to her daughter, Angela. Dianna was always too damn tired to do anything special with Amy except for the daily necessities. A lot of lost, precious quality time substituted with guilt. Sometimes in the evenings, after Angela was put down to bed, and mom would sit and relax in her rocking chair. Her oldest child, Amy would climb up happily onto her mother's lap. Dianna would cuddle her close, while they rocked and sang songs together.

It would be some years later, when Amy was a sophomore in high school that Dianna would be able to spend the quality time and much needed time with her oldest daughter. The guilt-ridden years of the past could never be erased from Dianna's heart; but the words of wisdom handed down to Dianna from one of her Aunts helped: "Amy will remember and appreciate more, the things that you are able to do together now, as mother and daughter, in these her young adult years." These words Amy's mom tries to keep in mind and heart to help buffer the guilt that had always haunted her. But back then, as a young mother, all the support and words of consolation from family could not take away the growing guilt that Dianna was living and experiencing from those nightmarish years.

Also, the fact of seeing other mothers with their babies and little ones would always upset Dianna. She would cry from the stabbing pain of envy, sometimes so much that her husband Frank would get angry and upset with his wife. So Dianna soon found herself ignoring and avoiding any contact with friends and other acquaintances for a while.

For some time Frank and Dianna became somewhat isolated, a life style forced upon them, making the young parents blind and unaware of other situations within family and friends. They seemed to be living or existing in a cloud, laden vacuum. The parents were always exhausted, frustrated and so tense, that Dianna, herself felt like a stretched, rubber band ready to snap at any given moment.

As for her husband, Frank, he never really wanted to discuss, converse or even acknowledge about his daughter Angela's condition with his wife or anyone for that matter. He placed the situation so far back in his mind, because being the husband and father figure, Frank thought it was his responsibility or job to fix whatever was wrong and to solve that problem. But instead he felt only helpless, defeated, inadequate and insecure.

Just once Frank admitted to his wife, "I feel, like I am on the outside of the glass or window looking in, but just can not find a simple way to get in. I felt that there could be an answer to solve the problems or situations regarding my youngest daughter. Perhaps just the right doctor, the right one with the right answers would come along to help us with Angela or take all her health problems away. Just one particular physician to find just the right key in order to make Angela normal, like her big sister Amy. If that wasn't possible than maybe something perhaps like the right kind of medication prescribe in helping our daughter Angela. I had an extremely hard and difficult time with it all, the pressures and I totally refused to face the truth about the hard, cold facts."

So for a long time, Frank suppressed his feelings along with his emotions and buried himself in his work, working many long hours just trying to escape from the problems. But realizing later that running away was not going to be his answer. The answer would have to accept and face the problems about Angela and the situations at home together with his wife.

***

Because of the great amount of time involved with the constant care that Angela required, plus since there were no guarantees from Doctor Swynds or other physicians as to whether or not another child could be born to the parents normal or maybe the possibility of having a third baby like Angela or perhaps even much worse. So Frank opted to have a vasectomy.

Doctor Swynds had been quite candid with his patients, Frank and Dianna, very soon after Angela's conditions became apparent and worsened. He more than advised the young parents to take the necessary precautions to prevent another pregnancy, even if another child were to be born to them healthy and normal. But Frank and Dianna just wouldn't have the time, strength or finances to raise their family properly.

So after much debating, discussion and a lot of soul searching between husband and wife, together they decided not to have any more children. The young parents based their decision on the present needs of the family. Dianna shelved her hopes of ever having or giving a son to Frank. She wanted so very much to give her husband a son because the family name would continue. But to Frank this was not so important to try a third time for a boy. He felt comfortable with their decision not to have any more children. So her husband had the vasectomy to spare his wife from the physical and emotional trauma of her having a tubal surgery within the fallopian tube.

But, now when Dianna looks back, on a personal basis, their relationship as husband and wife was only strengthened from all of their problems, difficult situations and decisions made throughout over the years in their marriage. They were drawn so much closer together physically, emotionally and spiritually, so much that their faith grew stronger and also their realization for the need of God to be present within their married life and within their family life as well. Frank and Dianna became each other's best friend and supporter.

"WHY?"

January, 1976: hospital studies on eleven month old Angela's progress recorded that she is starting to use hands, watches brightly colored and moving objects, possible fear of the dark, sleeps with night light

***

The support that Dianna and Frank received from their parents and other family members helped the young couple through many difficult, troublesome, depressing and trying times or situations within their marriage and their daughter's health perplexities. Dianna remembered one distinct evening when her and Frank was returning home from visiting their daughter Angela at the hospital. They stopped in at her parent's home to retrieve Amy, the oldest to go back home because it was getting late, and Dianna needed to put her young daughter to bed.

Amy's grandparents heard a car pull into the driveway and her grandma went into the kitchen to look out the window. She saw that it was Amy's parents so she went to the back door, unlock it and opened the door for her daughter and son-in-law. Once they entered the kitchen, Dianna's mother walked over to both of them and gave each a comforting hug. She than stood in front of them and looked at the two, saying in a quiet but strong voice, "The two of you need to be strong now, for yourselves but also for both of your daughters. Keep your chins up and no matter what happens from here on, please always remember to be there for each other." Dianna looked over at her husband and in return he smiled and winked at his wife. Together husband and wife than looked back at the strong woman standing in front of them. They promised her that they would remember the advice given to them. The three of them left the kitchen and went into the family room where Amy and her grandpa were watching a program on the television and enjoying a bowl of ice cream.

Little Amy seeing that it was her parents, jumped off from the sofa and ran over to them. She was so very happy and excited that her mommy and daddy returned from the hospital. Amy asked if her little sister was all right and when she would be coming home in her inquisitive and concern voice. Mommy tried her hardest to answer her daughter without being so emotional because she did not want to break down and cry in front of everyone especially in front of her child. So in a positive voice she said to

Amy, "Some time soon, but first before your sister can come home, she needs a few more tests done in the hospital and also the doctors wants to be very sure that your sister will be just fine to go home." With that response from her mother, Amy responded with "All right" and climbed back up onto the sofa to sit between her parents.

Dianna's parents also inquired how their granddaughter was doing that evening, what kind of examinations that the doctors wanted for Angela to go under in regards to her health conditions. For they to were concerned about how much longer she would have to stay in the hospital. They were also very interested and worried about the young adults physical and mental status. Dianna's parents knew the toll of heavy stress and health burdens affecting one's own life. They experienced such burdens because of their raising two disabled daughters with muscular dystrophy.

After some time discussing about Angela and her hospital stay, Dianna's parents wanted to know if either of them wanted something to eat or drink. Both declined the kind offer because it was already getting late and Frank needed to get home because of work in the morning and Amy needed to go home for bed. Grandpa had explained that he and Amy had ice cream for their evening snack. Grandma only shook her head back and forth and smiled over at Amy's parents.

As Dianna stood up to leave for home, her father asked if she had just a few minutes to give him before leaving. He led his daughter into other room where some privacy could be given to both of them without any distractions. Once in the other room, her father put his arms around his daughter and gave her a hug. He then let go and stood looking down at her and said, "Dianna, I want you to know that God has chosen parents, for special children to bring into this world, to perform the necessary responsibilities in life for these children. Parents that He knows that will give love and the proper care for them. Honey, sometimes in life, we do not always know or understand things that happens to us at the time. Or perhaps we might even ask our self, why are these things happening to me? Why my children, my family? Maybe later in life, some time later Dianna, that you and Frank will understand or think that the two of you might have an answer for that big question. Why?" Dianna's father gave her another hug and a kiss and his teary eye daughter returned his kind and loving gestures.

Together they left the room and rejoined the others in the family room. Frank knew that his father-in-law probably wanted to talk with his wife in private about their youngest daughter. He was talking to Amy's grandma when Dianna and her father came back into the room. Frank looked up at his young wife and once again he smiled and winked at her, acknowledging her departure and his way of showing his affection and love to her and gratitude for her parents.

Later that night when the three of them returned home and after putting Amy to bed, Dianna shared with her husband what her father had said to her. Through the years, Dianna has often thought about that one particular evening at her parents' home. Her mom and dad have so much love for each other, showed in many and different ways in their marriage. They have a strong marriage soon of fifty-eight years. Not only that but they continue and continue to give of themselves to their eight children (one decease, fifth child, daughter), grandchildren and great-grandchildren.

Frank and Dianna have been very fortunate to have parents, through their young marriage to be given love, support and wisdom to helped them when being young parents, for it strengthen them through some very tough times. Even today Dianna's parents and Frank's mom continues to give their all to them and their two daughters and great-grandchildren.

Dianna remembers Nana once saying, "When Angela was a baby and growing up into a little girl, that child had so many physical problems and changes in her young life. I think she must be a "Heaven's Child" put on earth to give us so much love, joy, laughter, pleasure and what happiness she possibly can give for all of us."

SUSPICIONS

February 24, 1977 - March 4, 1977: hospital admittance and report: Acute bronchitis (inflammation of the mucus membrane that lines the bronchi or main air passages of the lungs; prolong and recurrent attacks causes gradual deterioration of the lungs), heart and lung rapid rate and rhythm, possible breath holding episodes of no significance, probable convulsive disorder and nose mucoidal, rhinoscopy (examination of the inflammation of the mucus of the membrane of the nose), medication-phenobarbital (anti-convulsant, possible side effects are drowsiness, restlessness, confusion)

Angela able to reach out for objects and grab at, transfer from one hand to the other, continuous tics on face with jerky, wandering movements of both hands. Started wearing hearing aid around two years of age, with approximately eighty percent hearing loss. Several appointments with eye specialists, wears patch across right eye. Angela has a coloboma of the left iris, and microtomic of the left eye; has myopic astigmatism (defect of a lens that prevents focusing of sharp, distinct images or objects), but not a large amount.

***

Angela was constantly being taken to her specialists for having bronchitis attacks. The doctors would prescribe for her over-the-counter cough syrups, various tried prescriptions for medication to help control Angela's convulsions, seizures and her bronchial attacks. At home her mother had the vaporizer (cold air mist), in use for her daughter at bedtime or during the day if necessary.

Through the constant reminders from the doctors or nurses how important to perform the postural drainage percussion at home or wherever they happened to be if Angela's lungs started to fill up with fluid. There were times when the parents had Nana or grandma taking care of the children, Frank and Dianna would leave the house for a little while or perhaps take the two girls to their parents houses, that the two grandparents knew how to give the proper and essential care for their grandchild.

On top of all of those numerous medical problems that the young parents had to endure with their youngest, the first year and one-half of her life, Dianna had also suspected for many months a possibility that her daughter might not be able to hear. But although Dianna had voiced her suspicions on various occasions to her husband and her daughter's specialists about her concerns with this matter. She was answered with indifference in a way of a "wait and see attitude, or "too soon to confirm". Generally both Frank and the doctors made Dianna feel like she was looking for things that were not there or present within her daughter's health situation. Dianna although had justified her suspicions rationally, because knowing that neither her daughter's doctors spent the time caring and observing Angela on a twenty-four hour daily basis like the mother.

Dianna will always remember the very first time that she became aware of her suspicions. It was when Angela was nearly three months old. Dianna's sister Deb and her husband stopped by late one afternoon to visit with the family. Angela was fast to sleep on her parent's bed. Aunt Deb and her husband wanted to peek in on their little niece, so the four of them, aunt and uncle, daddy and mommy stood around the bed talking softly at first. But as the conversation continued, Dianna noticed that her sister's husband was speaking louder and mom glanced down at her baby, wondering if she would wake up from his loud voice.

As the three of them continued with their conversation next to the bed, all of them talking much louder, Dianna stood there at the other side of the bed observing her daughter, waiting and hoping for some sign or reaction from the baby because of the disturbances or noise that was present within the room. But nothing! Her precious little one just rested perfectly still upon the bed.

Dianna felt a sharp pain in her chest and her mind started to whirl with all kinds of thoughts, questions and feelings as to "why" and "what's happening here?" She glanced over to her husband who was listening to his brother-in-law discussing some matter and the whole time he was talking in a loud voice. Dianna's sister was also laughing and talking with her husband, even Frank would join in on the conversation that seemed to have the three of them so engross with whatever the topic was at that time. Mom stood there watching her baby, never joining in with the rest, just standing, glancing from one to the other and down at her little one quite asleep on the bed.

Dianna felt within her chest that something was not right. Her right hand gripped her left fingers and she started to breath harder. Mom told herself to calm down and tried to get her sister's attention. Her sister while still talking looked over at Dianna and gave her a warm smile. Dianna did not return the gesture but swiftly mentioned that Angela didn't seem to be responding to all the vocal noises within the bedroom. But her sister responded, "Oh Di, she's fine, stop looking for things that are not there. Sometimes loud noises don't seem to bother babies." In her heart mom prayed that what her sister said was true and than asked God to let her baby be all right, for in her heart she truly felt that something was wrong, not right.

✶✶✶

Some months later, Dianna's suspicions were confirmed one day when Amy and her mommy were playing records on the family's old stereo. Angela was quietly lying down on the floor in front of the speaker seemingly unaware of the sound that was being emitted from the stereo speaker.

All of a sudden without thinking or a moment's hesitation, Dianna jumped up and ran into the kitchen grabbing a metal pan and a large metal spoon and ran back into the living room. Standing behind her at some distance away from her daughter, Dianna proceeded to bang the utensils together creating a loud clanging noise. She moved a little closer, but not allowing her youngest to see where she was at, again Dianna bang and clang the items again and again. Amy asked her mommy what she was doing? Dianna explained that she wanted to see what kind of noise the two items created. Once more she moved even closer to Angela and continued with the clanging and banging near her daughter's ears. No reaction! Nothing!

Forgetting that Amy was in the room with her, Dianna started to cry while screaming, "Angela, you can't hear! I know you can't hear!" Mother's hysterical actions caused Amy to start crying and asking, "Mommy, what's wrong? What's wrong? Why are you crying? Don't you like the noises that you are making?" Shocked and realizing what had just taken place in the living room, mommy told Amy that it wasn't the noises but something else that was bothering her. She apologized to her oldest daughter, promised that she would be more careful as to not upset or frighten her again, and than placing a kiss upon Amy's cheek and giving a gentle hug.

Mommy sat down on the floor next to Angela and with a loving touch upon her baby's cheek whispered to herself and God, "Please let my baby be all right. Please God, don't let this be possible, don't let this be real, don't let this be happening to Angela, to us, my family don't need this problem right now, God." Secretly Dianna wept and within her chest a heavy ache or pain found its way that would only linger and stay.

When Dianna's husband, Frank returned home that evening from work, Dianna was still very much upset and concerned what took place earlier on that day. After the incident she tried very hard not to cry or show any emotions that would cause Amy to cry, be upset or even worry. At a young age Amy was already showing signs of maturing into a little girl that would worry about everything too soon.

Dianna went through the rest of the afternoon in a daze or disbelief, but at the same time in a somewhat normal fashion or front because of her children. She made supper with the help of her daughter Amy. Together the two of them set the table and cared for Angela, while Amy's mom watched the clock tick slowly by waiting for her husband to come home. Once Frank was home she immediately explained to him what happened with the music and the experiment with the metal pan and spoons. But Frank didn't want to believe anything that his wife was saying to him in regards to his little daughter not hearing the noises. Proof he wanted some kind of proof!

Angela was sitting propped up with baby blankets in her walker. She was in the living room with her back toward her parents. Frank instructed his wife and Amy to stay in the dinning room. He went out into the kitchen and returned with a metal pan and several utensils. Frank quietly stepped up behind Angela who was still sitting in her walker staring ahead of herself. For several seconds he banged very loudly the utensils against the metal pan and watching for some kind of a reaction from his daughter. Again he repeated the banging upon the pan. While banging on the metal pan the second time around again he was still looking for a response.

Then the clanging noise stopped abruptly, his arms dropped to his sides, his head turned from side to side and he stood there motionless a few seconds longer before turning around to look at his distraught wife with a stunned disbelief look on his face. With shoulders drooping, he walked back into the dining room, his eyes already misting with tears and said calmly, "Di, you probably should make a doctor's appointment tomorrow for Angela." He then grabbed his wife and the two of them stood there holding tightly to each other weeping.

Amy walked over to her parents and looked up and said, "Why are you crying?" Dianna glanced down at her daughter and Frank walked away into the bedroom. Mommy spoke to Amy in a shaky voice that her and daddy was crying because they perhaps thought that maybe her little sister could not hear. Tomorrow she would have to make a doctor's appointment for her sister. They would find out if Angela could hear or not. Amy had asked if her sister would have to go to the hospital again. Mommy said no to her daughter's question about Angela not going to the hospital the next day.

So the very next morning, Dianna placed a telephone call to Angela's specialist and was told to bring her in that very afternoon. Because Frank could not get off work for the appointment, Dianna had called her mother the evening before and informed her what had happened that day. She inquired if her mother could accompany her and the girls for the appointment when scheduled. After hanging up with the office that morning, Dianna called her mother to see if she would be free that afternoon.

Dianna would always be grateful and thankful for her mother's accompaniment that day. Because on that day, Dianna needed her mother's strength and courage to get herself through another episode of Angela's never-ending health problems. Dianna's mother could relate, understand and sympathize with what the family have been going through with her granddaughter. She raised and cared for two daughters (oldest and younger daughters) with Muscular Dystrophy. The youngest daughter died in 1968, at the age of ten succumbing to pneumonia and other complications related to the disease.

***

Dianna was fourteen and in the eighth grade. Her lasting memories of her younger sister are mostly those of pain and suffering that she endured through the many attacks of pneumonia, surgeries and the heavy, confining back and leg braces that she had to wear daily. How she struggled just to stand with those braces on, perspiring and never achieving the ability to ever walk in them.

One of the few good memories that Dianna cherish is with her sister Nan how the two of them would play Barbie dolls together for hours. For this was one of the few play activities that she was physically capable of participating in. But still Nan had no strength in her hands to pull on the outfits along with the snapping or buttoning involve. No matter what kind of activity Nan always needed some kind of help or assistance. But this did not matter to her siblings, the family played together and had fun!

Dianna remembers a night when her father carried Nan upstairs to the bedroom, so the two of them could have a pajama party together. The two sisters played dolls for a short while before their mother came upstairs to put Nan in bed with her sister. The cherished memory always etched in Dianna's thoughts when ever thinking of that night. Such a happy time back then, and a wonderful, excited and loving expression upon her sister's face. That same physical appearance that sometimes Dianna sees today on Angela's face, and sense that same excitement when Amy does something special for her little sister.

Dianna also remembers a time one month after Nan's death, she took their Barbie dolls in their zipped bag downstairs to the kitchen table, where Nan and her had played dolls for many hours on end. Sitting there all alone at her usual spot at the table, Dianna took out of the bag the two dolls that her and Nan had played with the most. Barbie and Midge. The girls would sometimes argue over who would get the Midge doll, which in both of their opinion was the prettier of the two. The majority of the time, big sister would let Nan have the Midge doll.

Dianna held this particular doll in her hands just starring at it. Looking over at the empty kitchen chair that her sister would have sat, Dianna felt such a sense of great loss. Quietly and quickly she put the dolls back into the bag and zipped it up for the last time. The bag was stored away for further use by her daughter some day.

***

Nine years later, Dianna and her mother are there together at the doctor's office with her two daughters Amy and Angela.

Together the two women sit in the room, one older, strong and wise. The other young, frighten and unknowledgeable of many things in her young life. Amy sat on her grandmother's lap while Angela sat on the examining table with her mom standing next to it. The two anxious mothers waited somewhat quietly and nervously together waiting for the verdict.

Inside the examining room the doctor took a large, metal, bedpan and dropped it on the floor behind his patient who was sitting on the examining table. He did this several times without any reactions from Angela. Dianna stood next to the table with her head bent forward while the tears flowed down her cheeks. She picked up her head and looked up at Angela's doctor. He placed a hand on his patient's shoulder and said with such compassion in his voice, while his face also showed the pain to give the statement, "I think you are right, mom. It is very apparent that your daughter has a hearing problem."

The last thing Dianna remembers was looking over at her mother, who had been sitting on the side of the room holding Amy on her lap, and quietly observing. Her head slightly lowered and her shoulders slumped a bit, weeping silently, a picture of defeat. Perhaps all the things happening to her granddaughter might have brought back memories to her of her own daughter Nan, whom Dianna's mother often remarked how much Angela resembled. But, just as quickly as she lost her composure, Dianna's mom pulled herself together and got her daughter through the rest of the afternoon.

Amy whom so young and not truly understanding what took place in that room on that day. Her mother at best talked with her daughter that night to help her try to understand the possibility that her baby sister was having a hard time in hearing things around her. Why the doctor dropped the heavy metal pan on the floor.

The doctor recommended that Dianna make an appointment as soon as possible with an audiologist downtown to have Angela's hearing evaluated. So Frank asked his boss for permission to take some time off work. He than mentioned to his wife that he wanted, insisted and was able to attend the appointment. Dianna made the appointment and together the three of them went downtown for their daughter's designated time.

At the first session with the audiologist, the young gentleman suggested to Dianna to hold her daughter on her lap inside the hearing booth. Frank sat outside with the specialist to help with the observations of Angela's reactions. Dianna was instructed to sit very, very still, so not to distract her daughter. He also warned the mother that some of the sounds would be extremely loud and that in all probability, a headache could develop afterwards.

He was right! Dianna found it very difficult to contain herself from wincing at the extremely high ear piercing noises or even from jumping at the variables in sound level. She tried to concentrate by watching her husband's reactions through the observation window as the father observed his little girl. The look of despair in his eyes told Dianna all that she needed to know even before the audiologist met with them afterwards to report the hearing results. So there the mother sat in the testing booth trying to control her reactions. Her head started to pound while her precious daughter completely oblivious to the sounds encompassing around the two of them in the small booth.

Later what seemed like an eternity the four of them met in another room down the hall to discuss the findings of Angela's hearing test; and what the parents now would have to do in order to help their youngest daughter communicate or be able to live life as a non-hearing person in a hearing world. He reported about an eighty percent hearing loss and gave the name and address of where the young parents could purchase the proper equipment or hearing aid or aids, and also the location to have ear molds fitted and made.

Then the parents were advised or suggestion given to apply for schooling immediately. Both mother and father were unaware of any schooling available for children that young. After giving the name of the school to contact, the gentleman requested from Angela's parents not to use his name or mention that he recommended this school for their daughter. Even today, older and a little wiser, Angela's parents never really understood "why" he mentioned that and "why" they couldn't use his name or that he recommended that particular school. But sometimes in life people say things or try to help others by taking a chance that it doesn't jeopardize their position at work. For various and personal reasons that audiologist made the decision to help and give information to that young couple that day.

***

Dianna made an appointment downtown on a Saturday so her husband could be with her for their daughter's first hearing aid fitting. This was an area in life that was new, uninformative, anxious and another health and medical situation for Angela that had to be explored. There were to be in the future many times when the father was unable to go because of his work.

So Dianna would engage others like her mother, her husband's mother or sisters to help with both girls. Amy went along also because she needed to know and understand her sister's way of life. She was a good girl to take places and sometimes even a big sister can help a younger one. There were times when Amy helped to make mom and her little sister feel good, give support and always made it a fun or adventurous trip downtown to either make or pick up the already made ear molds.

Angela would always sit on her mother's lap because she was afraid and unsettled when having the ear molds remade. An older couple owned the business and they were very caring, understanding and patient. Before placing any of the material for the mold within her ears, they would allow Angela to examine and touch it first. After that they would instruct mom to place her daughter's head gently and properly down upon a table. Then slowly they would work the soft wax within each ear creating an impression of Angela's inner ears. Amy would stand within range to watch and give comfort and reassurance to her little sister. This procedure was repeated several times each year because of the growth factor.

***

Also throughout Angela's school years there were numerous up to date hearing examinations done at a nearby junior high school. Sometimes mom would take time off from wok or arrange to go in later, depending on the time appointment. Dianna's mother, or other family members accompanied on several of those occasions to the audiologist. Amy went along also or was attending school.

Insurance would not cover for Angela's hearing aid, molds, batteries, y cord and the harness. They could not get any outside funding from any organizations because Frank had steady employment and Angela had so many physical problems that no, one, organization or group would claim her. So in order to financially meet those medical expenses, Dianna had to find a job.

She obtained a position as a mailing clerk at a local pharmaceutical manufacturing center working second shift, 5:00 P.M. until 1:00 A.M. These hours gave her the flexibility to care for the girls in the morning and get them ready and off to school, housework and the meals prepared so that Frank could take over when she left for work. Frank insisted about retiring to bed after his wife returned home from work. This meant that the both of them properly received about four hours of rest.

There were times when Dianna was so awake or restless from the job, that it was just too impossible for her to fall asleep right away. She kept this job about three years until the pressures of family, home and work took a toll on her health and finally decided to stay at home and care for her family. As her younger daughter grew older, her needs and health problems became increasingly demanding. But once again the financial burden soon outweighed everything.

***

145

MIMI BROWN

Dianna constantly heard, felt the weight or burden with paying the bills, forever continually always feeling guilty, that she could not help with the income. She struggled within herself whether or not to find employment again or continue to stay at home to care for her family. Dianna would discuss the issue with her husband and he favored her to return to work. Some family members voiced their opinions that she needed to stay at home. So Dianna felt pressured about resuming work outside of the home. She felt the guilt of not being at home to care for her daughters, too damn exhausted from working another job and heard from others that she needed to be at home.

As an example with the expense of their daughter's medical appliances in 1977, the one set of the hearing aid cost the young parents seven hundred and fifty dollars, molds cost fifty dollars individually and the actual pieces were thirty dollars individually. The harness for the hearing aid was approximately twenty dollars. Often the hearing aid would come apart or lose pieces in which these items had to be replaced. The parents were not able or financially able to purchase the double hearing aid, that was required for their daughter to wear.

Angela as a small child never really wanted to wear the hearing aid probably because years later her parents found out that she was profoundly deaf, and a hearing aid was not ever going to help her. Perhaps that explains "why" she never reacted to the loud squealing feedback noise. This loud sound would occur when the volume was turned up too loud or the molds were not in correctly. And "why" she was so agitated, frustrated and took the hearing aid apart or would lose those certain parts. Those always had to be replaced.

At times the parents had to send the whole hearing aid into the repair shop for cleaning, because Angela would drop food on it or spill liquids onto or into the aid. Once she got very upset, because she refused to wear the aid and dropped the whole thing into the toilet! Angela certainly had a creative way and much satisfying feeling about getting rid of the obstacle in her life. But what a costly repair!

Now when the parents think back, the aid probably might not had been a real help for their daughter, but only a burden to add to all the other burdens or problems in her young life. But at the time her mother and father thought they were doing the right means in aiding the communication skills. After all they were only following instructions from the doctors and other specialists.

***

During those years Angela was wearing her hearing aid, Dianna had attended sign language classes. She received a certificate for a beginner's class and two intermediate courses. Why two? Because mom received a good taste of what it was truly like to live or communicate in a world of silence.

Dianna's instructor for the intermediate course was a man who was profoundly deaf. The first class went right over her head! It was a whole new form of language for Dianna to learn. The first step into the classroom and right through the three hours not a word to be spoken by mouth or voice, unless one did it in sign. Mom got real good at signing phrases such as "sorry, repeat again, please" or " what, understand no" and " slow down, one more time." The second time around mom started to do better and even understood some jokes during class time, along with some few swear words in the process.

But most important with this tool of knowledge, Dianna was able to help her youngest one to communicate along with the rest of the family. Later, Frank took a class in sign language and Amy learned from her parents. Frank and Dianna felt communication was very important right from Angela's early years, because the school system only concentrated on her fine motor skills.

Angela's parents taught her over three hundred signs for names of family members, foods, items of clothing, household items of each room, different kinds of transportation and signs for feelings such as sad, happy, love, angry and sick. The two signs for happy and love, Angela constantly uses even to this day.

But their youngest one had still another problem to contend with along with wearing the hearing aid. She had numerous visits to the eye specialist in which Dianna's mother and her sister-in-law would accompany to help with the girls and many times just for support to offer. There too, Angela would become very frighten and would lose control of herself, by crying or throwing herself to the floor within the waiting room and the examination room. With much signing and patience on both parent and the doctor, they managed to get through her eye examinations.

Now not only the hearing aid that she had to wear, but also an eye patch that covered her right good eye. She wore this patch several hours each day to help strengthen the weak and undeveloped left eye. So wearing the hearing aid, patch and eye glasses, Angela was most of the time uncooperative, disturbed and an agitated child, who continuously tore off these items out of frustration. The parents certainly purchased and their daughter went through a whole lot of eye patches!

But Dianna understood after a while herself because one day she tried wearing just one patch over an eye. It wasn't easy to do when two eyes were always there to focus and see. Again mom had another taste of what kind of life her daughter was living.

***

One time out of desperation and the lack of money, Dianna along with the help from Betty concocted a plan to replace a pair of Angela's glasses for free. Over the years the parents had been purchasing their family's eyeglasses at a local department store because of the care and quality, especially their guarantee of free replacement upon breakage. And with Angela, her parents had to use this guarantee a couple of different times.

However, this one particular occasion her glass lens had become so badly scratched and marred, the parents knew that the glasses were not doing their daughter any good in that marked up condition. The lens needed so very much to be replaced immediately. The problem was inefficient funds at all in order to purchase another pair of glasses. One way or another her glasses had to be replaced soon for wearing.

So, together Dianna and Betty devised a way to remedy that problem. Angela's eyeglasses would just have to meet with an uncontrollable accident. After much deliberation and consideration, the two women came up with a plan. Betty would place the eye ware under the front tire of Dianna's car and she would proceed to back over them. It didn't work! The glasses were still unbroken.

So Dianna attempted a few more times to break them by driving over forward and than backwards, while Betty stood in the street directing the driver which way to turn the steering wheel. But the front wheel of the car kept missing to run over the glasses. Perhaps it was the driver who just couldn't get the wheels properly lined up and they both became hysterical with laughter. Finally by the misguided directions and the driver's dumb luck, succeeded in driving over and breaking them into several pieces.

They quickly picked up the pieces and placed them into a plastic sandwich baggy; all the while wondering what the neighbors must be thinking of their "Lucy and Ethel" antics, for that's how the two women felt! Like they had just played out a scene from an old "I love Lucy" comedy.

Still laughing Angela's mom and her aunt got into the car and drove to the department store. They casually walked up to the optical center's counter as if nothing had happened earlier that day with the eye ware in the street. Dianna pulled the baggy with the broken eyeglasses out of her purse. Than she looked the saleslady right in the eye and handed the plastic baggy to the other woman and said, "my daughter had an accident with her glasses, she dropped them into the street and the school bus ran over them."

With that untruthful statement coming from Angela's mom, Angela's Aunt Betty felt the uncontrollable need to laugh; and had to walk away quickly but carefully from that particular area, so as not to draw attention to her self. So she pretended to browse around as if she too like a few others were looking at the different frames on display. Of course though with her back toward that ridiculous customer standing there giving such a sad story about her daughter's frames falling into the street. Than ending with the school bus driving over them to the sympathetic sales lady behind the counter.

All in all, Angela would receive a new pair of eyeglasses. But Betty's neighbors did see Lucy and Ethel that day out their side living room window that faced the street; and wondered the thought what was wrong or going on with their neighbor in the street for the longest time, along with that crazy driver behind the wheel!

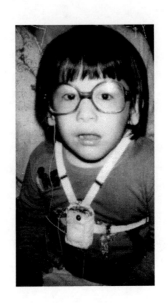

FIRST STEP - INTO EVERYTHING

Christmas Eve 1977: Angela Beth had her first step

Angela took her first step with her daddy and her big sister Amy at Nana and Papa's house. Frank felt and mentioned to everyone that it was like a miracle from above given to the family for a Christmas gift. One early evening while his father and him were watching the girls because mommy and Nana were out shopping. His little daughter scooted on her back across the floor in the dining room that had been turned into a family room temporary. An extra sofa and end table from the living room furniture was placed to make room for the Christmas tree.

Amy was playing on the floor with her sister and her dad and his father were sitting on the sofa talking. Angela pulled herself up from the floor by grabbing the end table. Frank was surprised to see her do that alone. But the biggest astonishment for all three was when Angela acted like standing at the table was not enough. Amy was standing not far from the table when her sister walked those first steps to grab at her hand. Everyone was so excited and happy.

A very special gift was given to this family that night. For the doctors told the parents that their daughter probably would never learn to walk. Such an accomplishment for a little girl to give her family a precious and memorable gift of complete happiness that was created by taking her first few steps.

***

1978: change of medication for seizures from Phenobarbital to Dilantin

1978: summer, plastic surgery to mouth because of a fall

By the time Angela was three years of age, she was climbing onto and getting into everything. Several times the family found her on top of the refrigerator to reach the cookie jar. Dianna remembered the first time she found the little girl there. Mom walked into the kitchen only to discover her daughter sitting on top of the apparatus with legs dangling while she munched away at the cookies. Angela behaved as if it was the normal thing to do. How she ever got up there no one knew? The only way was the chair to the stove onto the top. But there wasn't a chair near that apparatus either!

Still it was a comical sight though, barring the unsafe position young Angela was in. For there she sat, adorned in all her paraphernalia. She was a pretty picture of a little girl, a picture of love. Sitting up there wearing her glasses, patch and harness that contained the hearing aid. Mom's little nonchalant queen of the mountaintop!

Angela would constantly climb onto the kitchen counters or just anything up high in the house. Amy remembered a time when her younger sister had climbed up on a chair to reach the stove in order for her to light a cigarette. She walked into the kitchen and saw her sister sitting at the table smoking one of dad's cigarettes. She was blowing out the smoke from the cigarette like she was blowing through a straw.

Amy commented once to the family that Angela reminded her of a small monkey. Mom and dad agreed especially at the hospital when their daughter would climb over the railing of the crib. So the nurses eventually had to use a web netting over the top of her bed, which frustrated their patient very much.

***

Another incident had taken place one afternoon around 4:00 P.M., when his wife was at work and Frank was home caring for his two daughters. He was in the kitchen doing dishes and Angela was on the floor playing down by his feet. The telephone had rung and Frank walked away from the sink and went into the dining room to answer it. While talking and after a few minutes he heard a noise in the other room from which he had left. "I have to go!" He said into the receiver to the person on the other end of the phone call.

Frank hurried back into the kitchen and found his daughter standing precariously on one of the kitchen chairs. It was a Mediterranean style of raw iron with decorative scrollwork that sat above the top cushion. Angela stood facing the back of the chair with her mouth in an open position around the metal scroll.

Angela was at the opposite end of the table from her daddy leaning forward into the back of the chair. The piece of furniture was tilted and than before her father's eyes it tipped over. Desperately he tried to reach out with his hands for his little girl, but the table prevented the saving action. Angela had landed face down upon the floor with the raw iron penetrating her mouth.

Frank said he just panicked for the first few seconds after the incident.

When he finally gathered his senses and rushed around to the other side of the table to look down; was when he saw the blood and realized that his daughter was possibly seriously injured. He gently picked her up from the fallen chair and sat Angela on the floor. He immediately proceeded toward the sink and turned on the cold water. Angela's daddy took a clean cloth from one of the kitchen drawers and held it under the running cold water. He carefully placed the wet, cold dishcloth against her already swollen mouth. After a while he removed the cloth away from his daughter's mouth. That was when he noticed a deep gash above a tooth that was dangling.

His first instinct after seeing the damage to the inside of her mouth was to take his little girl to their dentist. But in order to do that, he had to find his older daughter Amy. So dad ran outside calling for the other sibling. He walked down the street calling Amy's name and finally located her running around with some neighborhood friends. The children where playing a game down the street several houses away in a big, empty parking lot. Dad yelled out her name and said, "Amy, get home now!" Her father quickly turned back and ran toward the direction of their house. Frank being so upset did not stay to explain to his older daughter what had happened and why the urgency sound in his voice.

Amy's first thought was, "What wrong? What did I do?" Amy later mentioned to her parents that she thought that dad was really angry with her. This was a place that was normally not allowed because her dad would not know where she would be, somewhat far from the house.

Angela had broken loose one of her front upper tooth. Frank seeing and realizing the severity of the injury to his daughter's mouth, made a quick and important decision to take her right over to their dentist office. Amy went with them to help give her sister comfort and assurance that everything would be al-right. It seemed that Amy had some kind of special affect on her younger sibling to control her when times of troubles or uncontrollable situations when regarding Angela.

Upon the examination the dentist decided and explained to Frank that he could take out the loose tooth but the rest of the upper mouth would require some needed surgery. So Frank with the two girls left the dental office and headed straight over to the nearest hospital emergency. The three of them waited somewhat patiently but nervously together in a room.

Finally one of the doctors came in with some extra help and instructed them to strap the patient down upon a board so he could examine the wound to her mouth. It looked so cruel to Frank as he stood there helplessly and watched all of them struggling with his youngest daughter as they carefully but physically strapped her to the board. But the patient's father rationalized with the fact that this was the only safe way the doctor could examine her.

In the meantime, Frank and Amy had stepped out to place a call to his mother. Nana immediately drove over to the hospital and sat with Amy in the waiting room. Her son was allowed to go back in the examining room to remain with the doctor, staff and his other daughter. He did not call his wife at that time because hoping not to upset her while at work. Frank felt that the accident to their daughter and the whole situation he alone without worrying his wife could handle the incident on his own.

After sometime waiting Nana decided for Amy's best interest to inform her son that it was better for the two of them to leave. She left the hospital with her granddaughter and drove back home to wait with Papa for the outcome.

The emergency physician explained to Frank that his daughter had cracked the upper part of her jaw and tore away the skin from the upper lip. Because of this kind of injury, the physician decided to call the family doctor to give the information in regards of the accident. It was not important according to the examining doctor to call Angela's specialist. For when he found out that the family's physician was the hospital's consulting doctor in charge, the necessary information could come from him in order to know what to do best for the patient.

Doctor Swynds answered the concerning questions from the emergency physician on call and suggested to him that plastic surgery was definitely needed for the patient. But he also felt and knew that there was no qualified plastic surgeon on at the time to handle the procedure. So Doctor Swynds made several other hospital phone calls around and in the area for the up most important matter at hand. Around 9:30 P.M. that evening, the doctor contacted Frank at the hospital to explain where, when and who would do the surgery.

Frank then called his wife at work around 10:00 P.M. and explained what had happened to their daughter earlier that day. Within thirty minutes after his phone call, Frank with Angela had picked Dianna up from work to drive across town. Once inside the car, mom looked over at her daughter sitting between her parents. She than glanced over at her husband and together they observed Angela who seemed unfeeling toward the injury to herself.

For there she sat happily in her car seat munching on an Oreo cookie giggling. How strange the parents thought that their daughter could eat anything at all? With her mouth in that condition! So very swollen and probably throbbing! Just looking at it for the mouth had to be hurting the poor little one. If anyone at all who looked distressful or in great pain that night, it certainly Dianna thought was her husband. It must had been one long afternoon and evening for him.

Once they arrived at the other hospital across town, the parents stayed with their daughter while they waited for the plastic surgeon. It was from this incident that mom and dad began to wonder or simply question if their little one could register pain? They had been curious for some time about this feeling since she rarely cried when hurt or in pain. For it was fear that seemed to always over power the physical suffering. This concern or question was brought to the surgeon's attention. He responded to the parents that he felt Angela had an unusually high pain tolerance considering how she was eating with damage to the mouth and upper jaw.

Dianna wished she could have drawn on some of that pain tolerance at that time to help herself through some of her own physical difficulties. For well over a year, she had been under doctor's care for severe back pain. At first her doctor felt that the problem to her back was brought on from all the stress, she had been going through concerning her youngest daughter.

But when Dianna's condition became much more aggravated and worsened, the x-rays showed a ruptured disk in her lower lumbar spine. Surgery was then required. But during her re-cooperation period, mom received lots of love and strength from her two girls and husband. She also had help and support from other certain family members. Soon dear old mom taking or thinking about her little family and how precious and strong, she was back on her feet taking care of them once again.

Mom tried to face each new day with hope and vigor, never knowing what could or would happen to her family. Many mornings she had to look toward the heavens to ask for strength. The girls' dad seemed strong at times. Why even her daughters just seemed strong in heart and at will.

***

But another frightful experience came later to shake up the family's strength. This time dad had to handle the apprehension alone without mom again because she was at work. He and Amy were going to play a board game called "Junk-Yard." The game had several pieces to it, one of which just happened to be a small steel ball. Amy and her dad started setting the board game up on the living room floor. Angela about four years of age was sitting nearby with them giggling while observing.

The two of them were ready to begin playing when Amy suddenly noticed that the little steel ball was missing. In unison daughter and dad immediately started to look over at Angela who had suddenly ceased her giggling and became very quiet. There she sat turning purple, with eyes wide open. Frank instantly knew where the steel ball was and his younger daughter was definitely not having one of her seizures!

Frank moved quickly and jumped up from his sitting position on the floor and grabbed Angela flipping her up side down. Holding onto her by the ankles, he then shook Amy's sister downward several times. The little steel ball plopped out of her mouth unto the floor rolling toward his other daughter who was sitting there, eyes and mouth wide open, clearly frightened and surprised by what had just happened.

All three people in the living room finally had calmed down after some time had past. Frank making sure that Angela was fine from the swallowing episode and Amy was all right witnessing with everything that had happened before her eyes. Dad and daughter thought it was time to begin the game and play, enjoy and have fun with the "Junk-Yard" game.

When mom arrived home that night from work, she inquired about their evening. "Oh, like any other night while you are at work." With that response coming from her husband, Dianna just had to know what now occurred while she was away from all of them. Perhaps it wasn't too bad because her husband seemed to be comfortable or maybe he was getting more adjusted to the unthinkable happenings.

His wife sat down on a chair across from her husband who was lying on the sofa. He sounded tired but confidently as the story unfolded to the children's mother who sat with her mouth opened and shaking her head back and forth. She listened intently without interrupting him and only questioned after he was finished talking about the game and the fun. Dad convinced and assured mom that their girls were just fine and in bed safely and asleep. Poor Frank, jokingly Dianna that night accused her husband of playing games while she was at work!

MORE STUDIES

February 28, 1979 admittance: respiratory distress, CT scans with brain work, seizures from birth, retarded growth and development, favorite play things at four are: stuff animals, boxes, musical radio, independent personality, learns by watching, fears people in white

***

Frank had to sometimes lie down on the narrow table with Angela through some of her scans because his daughter was so terrified of hospitals. There was even a time when mom had to stay right with her throughout her little girl's brain wave test. At the hospital the medical staff under doctor's instruction gave medication to their daughter in order for her to relax. The medication was given some time before the x-rays and other CT scans. But the older Angela was getting, the doctors had to increase the amount because she would fight the relaxation and simply refused to relax, sleep or even cooperate with the staff and complete the tests.

One time the amount of medication was increased twice after the first dosage. But still she would not relax or go to sleep. The nurse remarked, " We have given your daughter enough to knock out an elephant." So in order to get the necessary scans on Angela, Frank finally agreed to go through the scan with his daughter.

***

One of Angela's favorite toys for the hospital was a wind-up musical radio with different pictures of a nursery rhyme that would go around. She would wind it up and feel with her fingers and watch the pictures of a boy and girl in a rowboat go around with the tune of "Row, Row, Row Your Boat." She would carry this red and yellow radio with her constantly giggling all the while as mom, dad and daughter walked the children's hallways at the hospital. If the nurse was looking for the patient to give medication, they would only had to follow the sound of her radio in the hallway.

Her other favorite toy was Ernie, a stuffed Sesame Street doll, given at Christmas by Rich, a long life childhood friend of Frank. Dianna believed that with all of her daughter's hospital stays, the family had to replace Ernie at least four different times.

***

161

Angela would watch everything her family would do at home. She was a very observant child from a very early age. She was also an excellent mimicking child especially where her big sister was concerned. The strangest thing the parents noticed about her watching others was that she did not have to be facing them. Frank had always commented on her extraordinary peripheral vision.

Since the child always feared any hospital staff member who would be dressed in white. They would have to remove their lab coats during any procedure. Even at the doctor's office for her check ups they would remember and immediately remove their white jacket before entering the examining room. But as she got older and went to the doctor's office, the only person she was comfortable with and trusted was one out of the three specialists.

Through the years he had gained her confidence, trust and formed a good patient/doctor relationship. His two partners were also good with Angela, but sometimes they would still remove their jackets just to help make her feel more comfortable or at ease in the room during the examination appointment. Eventually the white lab coats were replaced with brightly different colored ones or fun looking patterns used at both on the children's floor at the hospital and at the doctor's office.

***

Inhalers were recommended to help ease her breathing difficulties, but because she didn't have the knowledge or capability to use them correctly, an air compressor was then recommended. It just so happened at this particular time that the parents were made aware of one that they could pick up one for free. The machine had been donated to a community service downtown by a family who recently had lost their child from a respiratory illness. A child's life was gone from an unknown family but another family was able to use that item.

Dianna thanked God for the aid that would help her daughter to breathe. She also prayed that God would help the family who had lost their precious child. That was the only expensive medical item that the parents ever received free for their daughter. Mom and dad both prayed and hope that they could help a child or person in need someday.

So Dianna was given a certain day and time to go downtown to pick up the small air compressor. The informer told mom the best time would be in the late morning or early afternoon. Once again she had to find someone to drive her and someone to stay with the girls. Since Frank could not take off any more time from work and he needed the car, Dianna asked her parents if they could help.

Her mother stayed with the girls at the house while her father drove the two of them downtown. After they got to the destination, they were given directions to a medical supply company. The company had cleaned the air compressor for the new owner. There they instructed mom how to use the machine along with the rest of the purchased and necessary equipment for her daughter. Mom had to purchase a mask for the face, plastic tubing and small container that would hold the two different kinds of medications for her little girl's breathing treatments.

Afterwards and before driving across town back for home, Dianna's dad asked if she was hungry? He wanted to know if coffee and donuts sounded good. Of course that sounded real good to both of them! This has always been a kind of a traditional thing with dad when you are out with him. It is coffee and donuts or maybe a sandwich with coffee. Oh, Dianna and her dad brought home some extra donuts!

***

July 11, 1979 - July 17, 1979 admittance: vomiting, stumbling, headaches possibly due to cyst on brain

July 12, hydrocephalus (a usually congenital condition in which an abnormal accumulation of fluid in the cerebral ventricles causes enlargement of the skull and compression of the brain), has become more pronounced as a cystic structure since last study of March of 1979, abnormal sleeping habits, never naps

***

The only way the parents would possibly know if Angela were experiencing a headache was by the method of observing and catching their daughter holding her head with her hand. Sometimes during her meals she would abruptly drop her utensils and lean her head down upon her hand. Then there were the many unexplained times while she was sitting or standing, their daughter would whine, or make strange crying sounds and want to lie down.

The doctor prescribed medication for sleep because she was so overly active and she was up continuously around the clock. She seemed never tired, never wanting to take a rest during the day but at the same time, she would be up all through the night. This did not appear normal and mom knew that her daughter had to get some rest or be able to sleep during the night.

So mom would give this mediation to Angela fifteen minutes before going to bed. She would have to be watched after the medication was administered because this would sometimes cause her to relax too much, almost to the point that she would lose body control. The parents were afraid that she could fall and harm herself.

***

September 14, 1979 admittance: stumbling, falling, and vomiting

An oversight between Angela's doctor and the office nurse caused her prescription for seizure control to be erroneously doubled. Even the pharmacist did not catch the mistake. She could not stand up to walk without stumbling and at one point she fell striking her head against the dining room wall. Her daughter also had been vomiting earlier that morning.

Dianna called the doctor's office and reported on her daughter's condition. She told the nurse on the other end of the phone how very frightened she was for her little girl. Angela was certainly not acting normal. Mom felt that there was something going on because she knew her daughter so well. The nurse on the other end of the phone call told Dianna to immediately bring her daughter right in to the office for the doctor to examine.

Once mom said thank you and good-bye, she than placed a call to her mother and explained the situation and where she would be taking Angela. Grandma offered to help and ride across town. Thanked God for a mother's help that day! Before leaving the house grandma had grabbed several towels and other items just in case if they were needed in the car. All the way to the office Angela had been vomiting.

When the three of them arrived at the doctor's office and knocked on the door as instructed, they were immediately ushered through another side door to an examining room. The doctor in charged that day examined his patient and suggested to mom that she should be admitted to the hospital for series of tests. So the three of them headed straight over for the admission. Later a call was placed to inform Frank what was going on and that he could pick Amy up from her aunt's house after work.

The result of this particular admittance and testing did verify that Angela had been over dosed with her seizure medication. Apparently, through some oversight between the doctor and his nurse, her prescription had been doubled accidentally. From that incident the parents would remember to question the doctor about their daughter's medications and dosage. They would check the filled prescription at the pharmacy.

For it was a human error but a very costly one. But most important that error was a dangerous, physical and emotional one that their daughter had to pay. In the future all prescriptions were question or examine by the parents before administering to either daughters.

ANOTHER SCARE

August 1982 admittance: pneumonia, seizure disorder

That summer of 82, seven years old Angela had been to the doctor's office and was being treated for a very bad cold. For several days Dianna had treated her daughter with different kinds of prescribed medications for the cold, running the vaporizer and trying to keep her chest clear by using the postural drainage method. Angela's mother had to watch closely for any tell tale signs of her developing a high fever, for if a high fever was to occur it would sometimes trigger a seizure.

One particular very warm August afternoon, Dianna was folding the family's laundry in the living room. Mom knew where her daughters were because she could her them in separate rooms. Every now and than she would stop folding and go into the other room to check on Angela. When she was not checking, she would try to keep an ear open for her youngest, who was sitting at the kitchen table entertaining herself by making her strange noises and giggling.

Amy was in the bedroom off from the kitchen with a girlfriend Sally, who lived a few doors down the street. Ten year old, Amy and her friend were discussing and making plans what they wanted to be when Halloween rolled around. Amy found some pink, sponge hair rollers and had become excited over a "cool" idea about using them to create a rabbit costume. Anxious to share the idea with mom she left Sally in the bedroom to discuss her future creation. But Amy through her excitement had forgotten the rollers, the main ingredient to the costume. She called to her girlfriend to bring the sponge curlers out into the living room.

Suddenly, Sally screamed, "Amy! Dianna! Come quick! Angie's!"

***

For Amy's friend upon entering the dining room had looked into the kitchen at Angela. She saw Amy's sister lying across two of the chairs. Sally surmised or thought that something might be wrong and walked over to the chairs and looked down at her friend's sister. She realized that the eyes upon the face were rolled back! The body was convulsing, along with the arms and legs spastically moving and at the same time, just like her brother would do! All of this plus Angela was vomiting.

Once Amy and her mother rushed and reached their kitchen doorway, mom could see that her youngest child was having a very severe seizure, in fact unlike any other before. Her oldest daughter looked alarmed and very frightened for her sister. Both girls wanted to help out even though the sight of seeing Angela in that state or condition was very troubling. Mom tried to think quickly without panicking or upsetting further the two girls. She needed to keep focus and her mind clear on what to do immediately for Amy's little sister. But this time the only thing she thought of was to call on Frank's sister for help.

Dianna immediately instructed her oldest child to phone the rescue squad and to place another call to her Aunt Betty. In the meantime, while waiting for the emergency help to arrive, mom and with the help of Sally positioned Angela so that she would not choke on her vomit. Dianna never felt so helpless as what to do at that very time and moment. Especially concerning her own child, who was uncontrollably convulsing and vomiting before her very eyes.

Mom kept praying for help to arrive quickly, for she was extremely frightened for her daughter's life. And, Amy and Sally, she just could not begin or imagine what was going through both of their minds that intense moment of time. The three of them standing near Angela, shaking, consoling and keeping her head turned to one side so the vomit could exit from the mouth properly into a black pan, the closet thing to grab used as a basin.

Within less than five minutes, Frank's sister, Betty arrived along with her two sons before the rescue squad. Dianna heard a voice calling out her name from the front door before she entered the family's living room. She was told that they were in the kitchen and it was all right for the three of them to enter. Perhaps the sound of her niece's voice over the phone told her enough to instruct her two sons that whatever they would encounter once arriving, that they themselves do not further upset or frighten their cousin Amy.

The three of them came into the kitchen probably a little nervous or anxious as what they would find or see, but they handled the whole intense moment very well. The two boys were there to give support to both of their cousins in whatever way possible considering their young ages. Dianna explained everything to Betty while they awaited the ambulance to arrive out front of her residence. The picture of the incident had been painted or drawn out about what had happened and took place to their niece and cousin.

Three people witnessing a very frightening experience, three people listening intently and one person performing the whole frightening and intense moments. For Angela was still vomiting and her body was stiff and rigid from the result of the seizure. The picture was grim and very unpleasant.

Betty had offered her assistance in what ever needed to be done for her niece. Her sons were with Amy, like big brothers and also her friend to help in any way they could as a child can do for another.

Time passed until the sound of the ambulance arrived and medical assistance could be given to their next patient. The doorbell rang, Dianna gave a sigh of relief and Betty gave a mixture look of concern, worry and support. Angela remained on her side across the kitchen chairs with the black pan under the side of her face. Dianna stooped in front of her daughter wiping her sweated face with a cool cloth given to use by Betty.

Amy went to the front door and let the paramedics in. For the next several minutes they took Angela's vitals, while they asked the mother the specifics of her statistics. Once getting Angela stabilized as possible, they informed the mother that her daughter would be transferred to a hospital.

They also advised her to ride up front in the rescue squad in order to keep them informed about Angela's life problems. Mom remembered the ride up front of the vehicle and intertwining her fingers while answering some questions of her daughter's medical history.

Dianna left Amy behind at the house to gather some things to spend the night with her aunt. Frank's sister knew that Dianna would probably be tied up most of the evening at the hospital with the youngest daughter. Always like before, Dianna knew that her oldest daughter would be in good hands. For Harry and Brad, who were like big brothers to the girls and would help Amy get through yet another very bad experience or episode with her little sister.

Amy said, "I remembered watching the rescue team strap Angela onto the stretcher. I was crying and screaming because it was the worst time I had seen her with a seizure. It really freaked me out so because at first I just didn't really know what was going on with her. I was frightened when the ambulance pulled away for the hospital and not knowing what would happen to my little sister."

***

Examinations - Interrogations

As was stated earlier, with every one of Angela's hospital admittances, she would have to go through a series of examinations in the emergency room and later more tests. Her parents were also subjected time after time to numerous, repetitive, grueling and exhausting sessions of questions of their daughter's life history from day one to the present time. These interrogation sessions (parents called them) would occur after their daughter was taken to the children's floor. The session of questions were conducted by the doctor on staff and also the various student interns who constantly proceeded in and out of Angela's room.

Both mom and dad dreaded these sessions because it made them feel so exposed to their personal life. Dianna would become very impatient and stressed out easily to the point of anger and frustration. Frank would control himself or keep everything in check and not lose his temper. He often times would remind his wife how important it was as parents to answer the questions in regards to their daughter. Dianna in return understood what her husband was saying but always ended up crying and than getting reprimanded again by her husband about losing control. She felt that their daughter was nothing more than a guinea pig, constantly being probed and studied like a lab experiment. That left the rest of the family feeling very stressed, exposed and vulnerable.

Always there were questions, but never any answers. And so these feelings that Dianna harbored deep within herself grew and were nurtured with every hospital stay. So one evening these emotions were reaped by a particular hotshot female intern as Dianna stood at Angela's bedside in the ICU unit.

Dianna had been there at the hospital alone for several hours and she was totally exhausted. She was up early that morning to get her husband off to work and spent some much needed quality time with her oldest before heading up to the hospital. By the time she would drop Amy over at her parents or Betty's house, the drive and then find a parking spot in the garage, it would be around late morning before arriving to the children's floor. She would spend a good part of the day with Angela, waiting for her husband. Frank had not arrived yet from work and would be checking on Amy at his sister's house.

The tall woman in a white lab coat came into the ICU unit briskly and had an air of over self-confidence and over bearing control, not only in her tone of voice but her whole mannerism. She stopped at the nurse's desk for a few minutes and after that headed straight over to Angela's bed. And for the next ten to fifteen minutes she shot questions at the patient's mother until Dianna couldn't think how to answer them anymore.

There at her daughter's bedside mom stood alone, drained, worried and believe it or not hungry, for Dianna had not had anything to eat since early morning. The in-turn was shooting one question after another and mom was feeling real tense from one answer to the next. For Dianna had gone through all this when her daughter was admitted to the children's floor.

The only thing that kept mom a little calm was to gently stroke her daughter's arm or hand. A few times during the interruption of questions, mom would give a motherly glance down at her little one to give a smile. For her daughter was so ill, pale and with so many IV's connected to her child along with the other medical items attached.

The doctor in training suggested that they leave the unit and go out into the hall to continue her consultation. She turned from the patient's bedside and headed straight and tall toward the double doors. Mom was very aware of the click-click sound of her shoes as they hit the floor with her fast, quick steps. Once more she looked down at her precious child lying so still upon the bed. Her small chest moving fast with quick, fast and short puffs of air. Before leaving the bedside mom whispered to her little one. " I will be right back. I won't be long."

She than left the bedside and walked over to the nurse who sat behind the desk. Dianna informed the nurse that she had to leave because the in-turn wished to confirm but she would not be gone long. The nurse gave a sympathetic smile and responded, "Angela will be just fine." After saying thank you to the nurse, Dianna slowly walked toward the double doors that led to the hallway of the pediatric floor. But before she gave the door a push, Dianna turned around to look at the bed that held her daughter. Once more she whispered, "I'll be back. Please God watch over my little girl."

Mom walked down the hallway where she found the woman in white waiting for her. In the hall were several different size wheelchairs and she found herself one and quickly sat down in it. She asked Dianna if she would like to sit but mom declined because she had no intention to be away from her daughter very long.

After about twenty more minutes or so of the interrogation of constant question after another, during which time Dianna's anger had grown to the breaking point. Feeling stressed and extremely exhausted from all the questions she just stopped answering the doctor to be in mid-sentence. Dianna stood perfectly still in front of the woman for a few seconds and than rubbed at the sides of her temples with both hands. When she stopped the messaging she looked up and stared at the other woman right in the eye.

The other woman in the white coat seemed to be somewhat comfortable and simply unaware of the young mother's distress. Dianna just could not answer any more questions and told her, "Stop it! I've had enough of this. I can't do this anymore! My child is lying in ICU, very ill and I am out here being drilled by you. I am going back to her bedside right now this very minute. Anything else that you might need for your notes, I suggest you look them up in Angela's hospital records from birth, because everything is there! Every admission, every problem, everything! It's all there!"

Dianna turned away from the doctor to be and left her sitting in the wheelchair. She swiftly walked down the hall toward the heavy doors. Instantly her right hand reached out and grabbed for the handle to pull open one of the wooden doors with re-found energy. Dianna walked back into the ICU to be with her daughter, who she promised that mom would return soon.

MIRACLE IN THE RAIN

Frank had remembered another time when the girls were eight and six years old, he and Amy had witness together a seizure Angela was having that day. That particular summer his wife had been employed at a nursing home as an aide, and that specific Saturday, Dianna had been scheduled to work the 6:30 A.M. to 3:30 P.M. shift. She had asked the nun in charge of the wing, all elderly men, in advance if possible for earlier hours for that particular day.

Dianna usually worked the later hours because it very much benefited her family. She truly enjoyed working in that area of the building because she cared for forty-two men. For it felt like she was giving loving care to forty-two grandpas'. The employee than had notified the Sister at the nursing facility one-month before and forward her request for the first shift on that weekend.

The family had planned a full week to adventure out on a camping trip with their good and dearest friends Ken and Sue, and their son and daughter, Scott and Christy who were close in ages as Amy and Angie. This was going to be the family's first vacation ever with the two girls. Frank and Dianna had never taken the girls anywhere too far away from their home or too far from a hospital in case Angela would have health problems.

Although the family did escape the day to day problems and stress at Frank's parents cottage in Michigan near a long and beautiful lake. There was plenty of ground to run and play, go for walks, fishing, shopping that both of the girls loved to do with their Nana. Also going down to the beach area that was only three roads down from the house. So this vacation of camping with the other family was definitely going to be a grand experience for them all!

When Ken and Sue had first invited their friends, Frank and Dianna, to go camping with them, mom and dad were somewhat hesitant because of Angela's bronchial condition. But, since their youngest daughter had not been hospitalized for any respiratory problems of late, the parents decided that it would be all right to join their friends after conferring with their daughter's physician.

Now both mothers of the young couple were very much concerned about them taking their granddaughter camping for a whole week! Nana was certainly worried and felt uneasy that the night air would cause Angela's bronchial asthma to flare up. She had good reason to believe and fear the cool night air might be a problem.

For up at the lake when Angela would be outdoors in the evening playing, in the swing or sitting near the campfire, mom would have to take her little girl back in the house after a short while because of her breathing condition. Many times when roasting marshmallows near the campfire would have to be cut short for Angela. She would develop seriously breathing difficulties and mom had to administered the breathing treatments.

First by using the small air compressor machine that was connected to a plastic tube connecting to a small plastic container filled with medication especially to treat the bronchial asthma. A plastic mask was connected to the top of the container and Angela wore around her face to inhale the medication to open up her lungs in order for her to breathe so much better. After that sometimes mom had to pound on her daughter's back to loosen the fluid in the lungs. So that was Nana's big worry.

Dianna's mother was altogether nagged about something entirely different. Her anxiety led to a fear that her daughter's youngest would wander away from the camp area and get herself lost in the woods! Grandma kept expressing the point about bears possibly in that area so far up north! But the parents had assured both of their mothers that everyone would be very careful. The time away from home was what they all really needed with their friends and would be so good for the four of them.

The two families had discussed and planned their departure from home and leave somewhat late in the afternoon. This camping trip would take about five hours of driving to the designation. They were all looking forward to a week way up north into Michigan to the Sand Dune Recreational Park.

Sue and Dianna would take the four children and drive in one vehicle with supplies while the guys would drive the van that hauled the two dune buggies along with other camping supplies. Ken had made his own buggy and borrowed another one from his brother for the trip up north. Frank with the girls were at home supposedly to be getting last minute things together in order for the family to leave when Dianna arrived home from work.

That August Saturday morning started out overcast and rainy. It was after 9:00 A.M. and Angie was still asleep in the bedroom. For that was really unusual for her to be sleeping in after seven. She was always an early bird and riser. Amy had just finished her breakfast and joined her father in the living room where Frank and been half watching and listening to a "Faith Program" on the television.

He vaguely remembered the spoke person on the program talking about testing one's true faith during times of need and trouble. And how if you truly believe then God will give you the strength and knowledge to get you through your trials and tribulations.

Amy soon became bored with the presentation on the channel and decided to leave the living room and go back to her bedroom. There she could check on her sleepy head sister and finish getting the rest of her things together and packed for the trip. But, upon entering the shared bedroom, Amy immediately discovered that her little sister was having a seizure while she lain there in the bottom bunk of the beds. The oldest daughter shouted with alarm in her voice for dad to come right away.

Frank immediately rushed into the girl's bedroom without any hesitation because of Amy's terrifying call. From viewing his youngest upon the bed he definitely realized that she was cyanic. He took in the still and stiff form of his daughter upon the bed. Dad noticed that her eyes had rolled back showing the whites. Also mouth gaped along with her limbs very rigid. He looked closely into the face had saw that she had bitten the inside of her cheek and tongue. His first instinct was to stay calm first for Amy standing so closely by and frighten for her little sister and secondly thinking what to do in the necessary care for Angela.

Frank asked Amy to bring him a washcloth from the linen closet that was in the hallway a short pace from the girl's bedroom. Then for some unknown reason Frank took the washcloth and left the bedroom and headed for the front door. He quickly opened the screen door and went outside onto the porch. There the man stood near the top steps holding the small cloth out under the rain.

He then turned around and walked back into the house and re-entered into the girl's small bedroom clutching the rain soaked washcloth and gently, lovingly placed it across his daughter's forehead. Angie started to respond coming out of her seizure. Calmly and quietly dad and help from the concerned oldest, together the two of them had administered to Angela.

For Frank it seemed like that rain soaked cloth had worked a very special miracle. Like an answer from above as he lovingly cared for his little girl the words from the television "Faith Program" came to his mind.

As for the family's camping trip, well they were able to go after mom had checked with Angie's doctor. Everyone had an enjoyable time swimming, playing in the sand, riding the sand buggies, roasted marshmallows around a campfire and just relaxing. Although Angie was not pleased about when mom and Sue moved her in the small chair out into the water of Lake Michigan. On that day Angela wanted no part of the waves to get her feet and bottom wet! She made a disgusted face along with some aggravated and grunted vocal noises.

But every morning mom and dad would wake up to find the youngest daughter just simply sitting outside the large tent in her lounge chair, enjoying nature's mornings and waiting patiently for the rest of the group to rise from their sleeping bags.

You know what? That little girl never once attempted to wander off, so our mother's worrying was for naught. Instead it was Frank and Ken who ended up getting themselves lost in the woods with the buggies. For they were on government land and were tress passing and asked to leave immediately by a forest ranger. Not Angela, she never wandered off and got lost!

PART THREE

Accomplishments and Education

Through all the youth years of Angela's trials and tribulations, there were some brighter moments. Special, short and indefinite intervals of times, when those brief happenings occurred to give hope and light to help the parents and their two daughters through those many dark and uncertain days. Those rare and treasured events in past time were the many achievements the youngest daughter was able to accomplish, through the constant effort, help, unselfishness, love and caring coming from that family four, of family, special friends and a few good schoolteachers.

Angela's best teacher and friend from the very beginning was her sister Amy, who with loving care and enduring patience taught her sister to do many unexpected skills. For instance, Amy worked very hard to show and instruct her sis how to roller-skate. The neighborhood girls would get together and skate up and down the sidewalks. Sometimes Angela would be outside on the front porch watching the activity that took place before her eyes.

Even though her sister would be busy playing with her girlfriends, she would always take time to stop and give some kind of attention or affection. Amy's friends would notice the sisterly exchanges of closeness and also stop to join in with giving some of their considerate feelings. Perhaps they would ask how to do some sign words, a gentle touch, hug or simply watching and imitating their friend's actions toward her sibling. Satisfy burst of giggles would erupt from Angela.

This kind of display for sisterly love and of friendship could be hard, could be uncomfortable or difficult, especially to someone different from themselves and if a person is not around others with disabilities. Fortunately though, Amy had a friend that lived two doors from her that also experience living with a disable brother. This life of family reality of living with disability situations with both girls helped others to become aware, accept, learn and be challenge with and in life.

***

So happened then one day, Amy took it upon herself to place the roller skates on Angie's shoes. She wanted to see if there was a possibility that maybe her sister would want to skate. What a surprise! There wasn't any hesitation on Angela's part to stand up and go for it! After a few minutes working very hard to get some kind of balance with her sister not to totter over but to just to stand up. Without the nervousness and shakiness, helping her to feel safe, secure by somewhat standing stable and upright on the ground.

The next adventure, though very important and really hopeful is the next step. Remember now, the new and inexperience skater has a vision defect and also deaf. So slowly and carefully the instructor must move her little sister to and onto the sidewalk! With painstaking time, effort on both and much patience on Amy, both sisters take the challenge! The task of skating had begun for Angela and a beautiful memory for Amy. One can only imagine how proud two sisters had felt that day. One had shown and given confidence for someone very special to perform a difficult but not an impossible task. The other received and felt the confidence to show the family and others her ability to perform such a difficult but possible the undertaking of skating.

But outdoor roller-skating wasn't the only thing that Amy taught her sister to do. One day the girls' mother was at home doing some needed and necessary cleaning upstairs in one of the bedrooms. Mom was called downstairs by the doorbell from one of Amy's friends. The message was to hurry and go down the street to the school's parking lot!

She found out from the girl that's where she could find her two daughters. Where? Why? What happened and why in hell were they down in the school parking lot, especially having Angela there! Mom's first instinct that something had gone very wrong! Perhaps her youngest had an outburst or behavioral problem and had given her sister a really hard, bad time. Even worse the sickening feeling that one of her daughters had been hurt. Sometimes Amy would have her little sister hang out with her friends and play in or outside but near the house. But not down the street in a parking lot!

When mother finally arrived at the scene out of breath from running, she soon discovered what the excitement was all about! Although she couldn't believe her own eyes what exactly she was truly seeing. At first it could not be possible, but a second or third glance told mom that it was a miracle or a very precious gift from God.

There in the middle of the parking lot mom saw Amy running with a big smile across her face along side of her bike! Running fast because on the seat steering the bike was the rider. Her little sister! Once again Amy had taught Angela to perform another difficult task. Really couldn't say who was the most proud at that moment. Mom who stood watching a beautiful and most rewarding picture of her two daughters together in the middle of a school's parking lot, the one running, helping and guiding or the one seated on the bike's seat.

For several minutes the scene took place as the rider peddled the bike and her sister kept it steady and the rider safe from falling off or hitting a few scattered small poles in the area. When the bike finally came to a stop with the help from big sister everyone exploded with happiness and enthusiasm. Mom signed to Angie, "good job" and "sister helped you"! A very excited, emotional and teary-eyed mom clapped her hands. She gave her little one a big hug and placed a kiss upon her cheek. Not forgetting the one responsible for this excitement, she finally turned to her eldest and gave her thanks, along with a loving hug.

One more thing that Angela had accomplished but once again her big sister was the important drive and force behind the accomplishment. Later that evening when dad arrived home from work, he too was given an unexpected surprise! And later that night mom gave her thanks to God for her two very special gifts.

***

Amy did other little things to help her sister such as matching colors when picking out her clothing to get dress, helping in the area of grooming oneself like brushing and styling hair and applying a small amount of makeup on her sister. Big sis at times would share some of her personal things or items with younger sis. But there were times when Angie wanted her sister to share more of her things that would make Amy upset or frustrated. Like any siblings the two of them had their moments.

But it was different because one had a very hard time understanding about situations in life especially trying to communicate where Angela could best contemplate and understand the issues or matters at hand. For Amy it was dealing with the ordinary and unordinary life family situations. But in reality for her and the family they lived in that abnormal or unsure, complicated and stressful family life style.

Whenever there would be friends over at the house playing or just hanging out together with Amy, they would give attention to Angela. The girls were always nice, caring and concerned about her welfare. They knew the closeness and love the two sisters had for each other. So they would befriend Angela and gave her time and respect. Amy had always shared her friends with her sister, besides it made Angela feel important or part of the group.

Sometimes when the girls spent an overnight Angela would join them, even though in the morning the girls couldn't find their socks or shoes. With Angela's fetish for those items, a person could come up short of a sock or shoe. But Amy was never embarrassed by her sister's condition. If a friend or acquaintance of Amy's had trouble or found it hard or impossible to accept Angela, or perhaps made fun of her, Amy found it hard to be their friend. She would lose respect for them or their friendship.

The times when kids can be cruel to someone different can cause great harm or pain. There were a few times when Amy got herself into arguments, disputes or fights with those who would make fun of her little sister. Amy was always and always would be little sister's best friend and protector.

When Amy was attending junior high, she tried out and participated in cheerleading. In the beginning of the season the girls from the squad would sometimes hold the practice sessions at Amy's house in the back yard. And of course the girls would have a small audience, like mom, the neighbors that lived next door and the biggest fan was Angela.

She would sit on the back porch steps and watch the girls do the routines. Whenever they would do any jumping, back flips or shake the pompoms she showed her delight by signing, "happy" followed by smiling or at times just simply giggling. After awhile the girls would take a brake by sitting down near Amy's sister showering her with lots of attention. If any of them knew signing there was some communication with Angela, some gave her hugs or whatever they felt comfortable with by their way of friendship.

Through all of the attentiveness she felt that the girls were her friends too. Big sister taught Angie how to hold and use the pom-poms, a gift from her sister. Angela had learned how to use the shakers and with help from Amy and the other girls, she could perform some small routines or simple movements. One thing for sure about Amy, she never gave up on her sister, she will always be there to love, guide or comfort, her sisterly friend.

***

Angela enjoyed another school activity attending some of the football and basketball games along with her parents. When Amy was a freshman and sophomore, the football games were held in late afternoon, before dad got off from work. So mom's sister, Aunt Deb, would pick her niece and sister up and the three of them rode together to the stadium. Sometimes grandpa and grandma would meet in the parking lot or everyone would meet up somewhere inside so the family could sit together.

Mom would usually pack a little brown bag snack for her daughter. This sack snack consisted of some kind of fruit, a peanut butter jelly sandwich and a small drink. Aunt Deb would usually buy her niece a small bag of her favorite candy, M & M's.

But, as Angela's behavior problems began materializing, first in the form of refusing to walk. At times though when walking was definitely not what she wanted to do, Angela would be agitated when told she had to walk. There were times when she refused or displayed her displeasure. Her bouts of anger with walking became actions of falling down hard on her knees, biting at her hands, slapping herself or swinging out her arms. Those actions are accompanied by unhappy vocal sounds.

Mom had to contained her emotional self in order to control her little girl. Angela's mother did this first by the means of communication through signing. Second, by using body and facial movements and expressions to help Angela to understand; and not allowing thoughts from other people, what they are seeing and hearing.

Mom received help from Aunt Deb, because she would bribe her niece to walk with a bag of M&M's. Most of the time those outbursts would not last too long because she knew where and what was eventually going to take place by mom's signing and Aunt Deb's treat. She would see and enjoy the football game and watch her big sister along with the other cheerleaders.

Angela knew later at half time, Amy along with some of her friends would find her in the stands. When the football game was finished, than it was time for Angela's walk out of the stadium. Back to the car was once again bribed by Aunt Deb with a bag of candy!

There is one particular funny incident that occurred at one of the football games, an incident that will always be remembered by the family. It was during the game when everyone had become so involved with the action on the field.

When mom had glanced over to check on her daughter. She was not sitting next to grandpa, who had said, "Let Angie sit here next to me on the bleacher. I'll keep an eye on her." "Right dad," mom had thought to herself while looking over at her mother and giving an unsure look.

A split second moment of panic from mom! Immediately she turned to scan the stands. Shock and surprised to find her daughter just a bleacher above. There sat Angela between two elderly men! With her legs crossed, intently watching the game, while simultaneously helping herself to their boxes of popcorn!

Relief, embarrassment and then humor had struck mom all at the same time. Angela's dad was quickly interrupted from the game by a quick nudge on his arm. The rest of the family, like Aunt Deb and the grandparents were informed to turn around and look behind them. For the scene behind was such a comical sight and everyone broke out in laughter. There sat the granddaughter sitting between two strangers nonchalantly munching away at their popcorn and giggling.

Gathering some composure mom signed to her daughter, "No!" "Sit down here, please." But the two elderly gentlemen responded back to mom. "She's not bothering us, it's all right. Besides she's helping us to eat our popcorn." And so that is where Angela sat for the rest of the game just giggling and munching. She was very happy with her new friends! Several times mother would check on her little one to make sure everything were fine. Once her little girl signed "happy" back to her mom or dad.

The other most favorite part of the game for Angela was during the half time. Why? That was when Amy and the other cheerleaders and some other friends would come up to visit with little sister in the stands. Certainly those young people had made Angela feel good and happy.

***

Other accomplishments and activities that Angela was able to achieve before the onslaught of her severe behavior problems were: learning and retaining through her parent's teachings of over three hundred sign words. Some of those words the child could actually print, as well as her name, until she shortened it by printing only two letters, by just using the initials AB. Today she just simply prints "Ang." She could recognize other sign words as well on paper or a chalkboard. The family taught her how to print the ABC's and numbers one through ten.

In fact, Angela's first sign word was "shoe" so ironic, for she always had a shoe fetish. Can one just imagine the unexpectedness and reality from the family? Especially when she had signed the words such as mom, dad and sister. Also two other sign words became very important in Angela's life, "happy and love."

She learned through the family's instructions how to use the appliances within the household, for instance, the washer-dryer and properly how to separate the clothing before the wash. She enjoyed folding the laundry and helping mom to put everything away immediately.

In the kitchen the unloading and reloading of the dishwasher. If someone just pulled out a cake mix, the little helper would get all the necessary items to perform and finish the task. She also wanted and insisted to help with the vacuuming. Swept by a very good job!

Angela enjoyed outings such as shopping, visiting family or friends. Over time the parents knew and tried to avoid large crowds because of their daughter's insecurities. Unfamiliar faces or places would cause rash behavioral changes. She would abuse herself by the way of hitting and biting. Sometimes Angela would want to find a place just to be totally alone.

She always enjoyed visits to or from the family. Time well spent with her grandparents, at Aunt Deb's house because of a large collie dog Misty, that Angela loved to rough around with and ride like a horse. Her Aunt Sandi, wheelchair bound, she felt comfortable with also, probably because some of her friends in school were in wheelchairs.

When the family would all get together, Dianna's sister-in-law, Judy would have her mother present, who was also deaf. So Angela received signing from all of them. But the niece would sometimes play a game with them by trying to ignore the sign language being signed to her.

There were others in her young life that she enjoyed spending time, like her Aunt Betty and Uncle Harry and their two sons. For they were fun, loving and it was like having two older brothers, in which both girls formed a strong bond.

Angela loved visiting and spending time with Nana and Papa at their cottage up in Michigan, along with her sister Amy, brotherly cousins, Harry and Brad, and with other friends. The children spent a lot of fun time down at the lake, playing up at the house, having the grandparents spoiling them and the evening marsh-mellow roast around the fire. Where everyone enjoyed the night fire in the country under the bright stars, which was made together by Papa and Frank. Just a simple dunged hole in the ground with a couple of wooden benches.

Angela also attended the day camp programs with other disabled children during the summers. At times she was reported as a happy and successful participant while other times were completely disastrous. There for a short while she had established a few good friends. Although the summers were always very difficult on her, especially when school was not in session.

***

Now when it came to teaching Angela about her personal hygiene, she was always willing and cooperative. For she never liked being unclean. Angela would constantly change her clothes several times a day. So, mom never had to struggle with bath times because both girls liked their bathing.

Through a lot of repetition of signing, patience, effort and help on everyone's part, she was able to learn how to care for herself. But one of mother's biggest concerns with her youngest before and when she would enter those puberty years. How mom would communicate enough for her to understand the bodily functions? Since Angela usually followed her mother into the bathroom, it was decided to allow her daughter observe the personal hygiene routine, especially when mom was having her menstrual cycle.

Communication by signing and observing to help her daughter fully understand that it was a natural body function. So someday Angela would know how to care for herself and do the necessity with little assistance.

Every evening before bedtime, Angela would put out her clothes for the following day. After all her bedtime preparations, she would descend the stairs once or twice more just to sign, "good night, love you" and than blow kisses to daddy and sister. It was also a way to stall the bedtime!

Once Angela was in bed, mom would sign to her "prayer time". Mom would always take her daughter's precious hands into her own and together they would sign, and pray, "Now mom lays Angie down to sleep." Then "good night, love you" would be exchanged. Several big and accepted hugging and kisses with lovingly arms wrapped tightly around one's neck and the vocal sound of "Aaah" into mom's ear. Before the light switch went off another exchange of "I love you" and kisses blown would fill the air. As mother descends the stairs, she enjoys listening to the happy giggles.

All those special things that Angela was taught how to do and enjoy doing, by the family soon came to an abrupt halt. When the behavioral problems took over the life, almost wiping out everything she had ever achieved.

✵✵✵

Schooling

As was mentioned earlier, the parents learned about a school for their daughter from an audiologist at her very first hearing test, when Angela was about eleven months old. It was a special school for the multi-handicapped or disabled children. The particular school was not far from their home, within the same area of town. In that educational center, the young parents and their youngest were enrolled in the Parent/Infant Program, from the month of September of 1976 to November of 1978.

The hourly sessions were held twice a week and most important to involve both parents. Back than when the father and mother were both working full time jobs. Dad's hours were days, 7:00 A.M. to 3:15 P.M. Mom's

working hours were different from her spouse. She reported to work at 4:
30 P.M. to 1:00 A.M. These hours gave dad the responsibility of caring
for their children and allowing them not to pay out for a baby sister.

Since Frank would not be allowed for time off or going in later for his
job from his employment, other arrangements had to be accommodated
for the classes. Dianna's employer after hearing the family situation about
their daughter and the necessary and much needed classes; agreed to allow
her to start work an hour later because the set up session began at 4:00
P.M.

So for the next two years the family attended the classes. The father
after getting off from work would directly go home and pick up his wife
and youngest daughter. Sometimes Amy would go along with her parents
and sister to attend the class. But there were times when Amy stayed with
her grandparents or another family member.

Angela being a very young student to attend these special classes. Because of her young age and the severe multi-handicaps or disabilities, the
school basically observed the family in a variety of experimental settings
such as in a playroom, kitchen, bedroom and a large motor room (muscle
development activity room).

The instructors were very caring and considerate of the family particular situation. Their instructions for the parents dealt mainly with communicative and functional skills. Along with facial expressions, body language and the proper use of voices just in case their daughter had the sense
of hearing with her device of the hearing aid. They were also instructed
how to properly perform the play skills.

These classes were a great help to the family especially for Amy because the parents wanted her to also feel important and comfortable in
helping her little sister. Sometimes though during observations from the
instructor made the parents feel a little uncomfortable.

With their oldest daughter, mom and dad never thought about the
ways of talking and playing, they just simply did these normal activities
with love and devotion. But with their youngest, they had to really focus
on using all the important skills in ways that would help and benefit their
daughter in a much different ways of communicating and teaching, and
still providing the love and devotion necessary for a child's development.

From there Angela went to another program at a different school.
She attended a schedule, somewhat like an early pre-school setting. This

particular class started in September of 1979 to June of 1980. Mom drove her to the classes that were provided several times a week.

Physical and occupational therapy services were given from the teachers. Once again because of Angela's multiple disabilities, the educators basically just observed and perhaps experimented with the child because at times they were too, lost how to really help. Sometimes mom had to just observe certain activities, while other times be included and allowed to join in with the interaction of teacher and her little girl.

There were days when mother felt good seeing maybe a small result with the class. Then there were days mom left with her little girl feeling empty, hopeless and helpless, with a great heaviness on her shoulders and within, that there had to be something more, something out there, better to help, educate one so young and with so many problems.

Toilet training was a positive and cooperative affair between the school and with mother. Since mom had always treated Angie as a normal child, she employed the same potting training techniques that had been used with Amy. It took a little longer amount of time but with patience and perseverance, it worked and prevailed! By the time Angela was four and one-half years old, she was toilet trained during the daytime with few daytime accidents.

At night she wore a diaper and continued to do so until the age of six. There was difficulty and resistance on her part during the bathroom visits during the night. But around the close age of seven to a little over eight years of age, Angela was completely and successfully toilet trained for both day and night, although a few accidents did occurred.

During her education at the preschool, the Board of Education suggested to the parents a school for the mentally retarded. But Frank and Dianna both refused, because no one had proven conclusively that their daughter would be unable to learn. Besides the parents felt and knew that she was learning at home through their love and patience.

Then from about the age of five and one-half to eight years of age, Angela went to another elementary public school, from September of 1980 to June of 1983, in a multi-handicapped class. She received speech/language and occupational therapy while attending that particular school. Educational goals included fine, gross motor skills development, reading readiness, language skills and increasing social skills.

Since her teacher was very aware of the fact that the parents had been instructing their daughter with sign language at home, she reinforced her student with speech and language goals. She also encouraged sound production, awareness of different sounds (lip movement and throat vibrations) and worked on increasing Angie's attention span.

The first year at this public school Angela's attitude was, "I'll do it when I am ready. Don't push me." When she is pushed, she in turn will tune the teachers out or anyone else for that matter. But by the second and third year, that student began to blossom and did very well through her instructor's love for her job, enduring patience and the special care given by both teacher and those of the classroom aids.

While Angela attended the school there, her classmates and along with other schools participated in an "Art Show" held at a local mall. Angie's flower design made of yarn won for her an award of a check for ten dollars.

During these years there were no major problems, but Angela was ahead of her classmates without enough challenges. So, her teacher felt because of her learning capabilities, that her student needed more challenges. Therefore, a different and another school placement was needed.

Next, Angela was placed in the multi-handicapped class at a public elementary school for the 1983-1984 school year. At this educational elementary center, the educational goals set up for Angie included areas of reading and math readiness, behavior, receptive and expressive language, that included using the language of signing. Occupational therapy goals were based on improving her attending to tasks, as well as in improving fine and gross motor skills.

List of known signs to Angela were accompanied by pictures and were presented to her, but she would respond to gestures than instead of formal signs. She was able to sort by color, shape and separate three objects. Other activities of interest were given such as including the skill of cutting with scissors, tracing and following simple directions on paper.

That first year at her new school was a slow process for Angie to adjust and adapt herself to her new teacher, classmates and surroundings. This public school was more restricted and confining than her last.

At the school before Angela was given more freedom with some responsibilities, making her feel needed and important; such as helping out in the class room with some set-ups, lending help to her classmates and taking notes and etc. from her teacher and aides to the office. At her new school she didn't have the little responsibilities and freedom that had once been allotted to her. The teacher did not believe that her student could be answerable to such duties.

Frank and Dianna both felt that Angela never accepted her new instructional environment. Although they didn't really notice any changes in their daughter's attitude or disposition at home, for she was her usual happy and extremely giggling self.

It was through the frequent meetings the parents had with their daughter's teacher, that they began picking up subtle hints and remarks to the fact that Angela wasn't adapting very well to this new school placement. It was constant and continual reports that her participation was limited and spontaneous. She was also reported to be passive and uninterested in her classroom activities of subject learning.

Then, suddenly without any warning, Angela started having uncontrollable voiding problems. Mother first noticed that she was bedwetting and in the morning her bed would be soaked. So, mom had to put a plastic liner on the mattress in order to protect it, along with the other covering. During the day at home, Angie would sign to her mom, "toilet", but by the time the two of them would reach the top of the landing, she would be leaving quite a trail of urine up the steps and into the bathroom.

The school also reported that Angela was having frequent accidents there during the day. So, mom had to send extra changes of clothing. Angie was even returning home and getting off the bus wet. Because of her unusual incontinence, mother made an appointment with Angela's doctor.

***

December I, 1983 - December 6, 1983 hospital admittance:

Voidance problems, voiding cystogram (a diagnostic procedure in which an x-ray of the bladder is obtained by injecting a solution visible on x-rays into the bladder)

The preliminary tests that were done in the doctor's office were too inconclusive, so hospital admittance was suggested for a complete urinary work-up. By now eight year old Angela was terrified of hospitals and doctors so much that mom along with her doctors, felt that it was necessary for mother to stay right with her daughter day and night, to aid the hospital staff in caring and communicating with the patient. The adolescent along with the parent were given a room at the very end of the hall for their privacy and so as not to disturb the other patients.

So, in December of 1983, Angela was diagnosed as having a neurogenic bladder (the nerves of the valves to the bladder would not operate at the same time, causing her not to be able to release all her urine at once). The doctors also reported that their patient had an overlarge bladder, which causes dribbling during the day as well as at nighttime when the bladder relaxes.

One of the hospital's doctors wanted the patient's mother to perform catheterization on her daughter several times during the day. But because with the inability to understand "why" along with the embarrassment for her daughter and the fear on mom's part of perhaps hurting or harming the physical aspect, mother said "No." For she knew that Angela would have fought against any and every attempt to catheterize. Just like the few times when suppositories were recommended by the doctor, as some relief for the daughter's occasional bouts with constipation. But other ways of laxatives were used.

So instead of that procedure mother taught her little one a relaxing method that could be perform while sitting on the toilet and just massaging the lower part of the abdomen. Usually that step would take place approximately about ten to fifteen minutes. Than the next step for her was to lean forward applying pressure to the lower abdomen. Therefore aiding the bladder in the action to release the urine. This relaxation technique felt by both parties involved was more comfortable than the other choice suggested by the doctor.

During that particular hospital stay for Angela, her sister Amy was away at winter camp along with other six graders. The day she was due home from camp, her parents were at the hospital for their other daughter. When Amy arrived at her school on the bus, she saw everyone's parents except for her own. Instead noticing that her Aunt Betty was there to await her arrival from camp. Amy mentioned later to her parents that she knew immediately sensed and knew that something definitely was wrong with her sister.

Frank's sister, Betty gently explained to her niece the reason "why?" Mom and dad were not able to take her home from school camp. The aunt had to explain about her niece's hospital admittance. But Amy would be going to see her sister later that afternoon. Dad had arranged with the nurses on the children's floor for permission for the older sister to visit. He explained to them that Amy had been away at camp. Also because the sisters were very close and the older would be very worried and concerned.

Thanks to the understanding of the hospital staff, they saw no reason that their young patient couldn't be allow some time with a sisterly visit. So, Aunt Betty drove her niece to the hospital and the two sisters were allowed a brief visit. Brief, but a moment in time when a special memory was carved and never forgotten. A time spent in hugs, kisses, a few tears, "I love you," in sign and the sound of happy giggles.

The next several months the family helped Angela to deal with the defect in her bladder. But, because of the daytime incontinency and the nighttime bed- wetting, Angela had to wear during the day special underpants that held an absorbent pad. And at night she would wear an adult type diapers. Twice a month, these items had to be ordered along with special bed protector pads from a local medical supply company. These items were very costly and were not covered by any insurance.

The child had no problem accepting and wearing the daytime protective garment, but getting her to wear the nighttime diaper was a problem. The mother sensed, saw and knew that her daughter felt embarrassed having to wear an article of clothing that resemble a diaper. She was very smart to know that babies wore these things.

Her mother would never forget the look on her little girl's face, when that first night Angela tried to sign to her mother "why?" It hurt mom so much to see in the tender eyes of a young girl that look of embarrassment, confusion and yes, even a look of anger in her teary brown eyes. Hard as it may have been the explanation with signing took place to try to restore some dignity back to that beautiful young girl.

So, each night mom had to struggle with her youngest to put on the protective bottom and every time the wearer would tear one or two up before finally submitting to her mother's insistence. In the beginning before the diapers were purchased, the parents tried arousing their daughter from sleep to use the bathroom. But she would become so combative, disoriented and abusive to herself that it was easier on all of them just to use the nighttime diapers. Even the doctors suggested and agreed after some lengthy discussion about the nighttime incontinence and solution to the use of the adult diaper.

This new problem for Angela what was diagnosed having a neurogenic bladder caused the beginning of the behavioral changes and self-abuse.

Her growing frustrations would start with the swinging out wildly with her left arm, smacking herself in the eye with her fists, biting both hands and banging her head on the wall, floor or any available, nearby object.

But with much patience and training, the smacking of oneself in the eye stopped for a little while. The parents and the other daughter would sign to Angela to let her know that it was wrong and it would also hurt and give her pain. So the family incorporated by using the sign and concept of anger when she was feeling and getting very frustrated and angry.

***

Once again the child's physician suggested to the mother, the idea of a "Home Placement" for the daughter. Again, Dianna responded, "No, I just couldn't do that. She is my daughter! I feel it's my, (our) responsibility to care for her. My husband is not here to respond about this suggestion. But I know deep in my heart what he would also say. The answer is not a home placement." The parents truly felt and believed with all the love, patience, work and perhaps maybe a miracle from God, their daughter would grow out of these changes going on within her life.

But at the same time in the back of mother's mind, she had pushed the real reality of this whole situation from coming forward. Dianna had given birth to Angela. The mother, it was she that was going to always give the love and care. Along with Frank and Amy. Not a total stranger! These thoughts and feelings led to a hard and very uncertain future.

***

The year of 1983 was extremely difficult for the family. Not only dealing with the daughter's medical and health problems, but Frank's new truck was stolen, his job folded and all of this was reflecting in the oldest daughter's attitude and school performance.

Dianna had spent so much of her time around the clock with her youngest child. That mom didn't give her eleven-year old daughter, Amy, the quality time that was needed from her mother.

So, 1983 ended with much uncertainty and doubt and 1984 arrived with the further deterioration in Angela's behavioral problems. Frank's unemployment lapsed after ten months and no permanent job prospects, so he took on various odd jobs, and the parents had exhausted their savings for a future move into buying a house. Dianna had guilt feelings for not doing enough for her family.

Once again she sought employment and finally obtained a job in the fall of the year, working as a teacher's aid with preschool children. She was lucky to have an employer to understand the family situations. The center allowed their employee to work hours that would be helpful for her family and beneficial to the pre-school center. Now Dianna was not only wife and a mom within the home but her life change from outside the home.

***

In August of 1984, Angela was seen for a formal evaluation, by an agency recommended by the public school board. There were two sessions held in our home. The first session included the instructor, mom and Amy. The big help came from Amy assisting her sister by signing and modeling tasks for imitate. The second time was the following month in September. That time was an evening appointment with the parents to give signs to their daughter to follow directions when working on simple tasks.

It was important for mom and dad to be present with Angela because she was very hesitant about accepting and working along with a stranger. Mom had to communicate by signing to her daughter because the examiner had limited signing skills. So communication between the woman and examinee was the first major problem. The parents immediately could see that Angela felt uneasy being around the uncommunicative stranger.

There was uneasiness with the woman because of her limited communicative skills. Mother never could understand why an examination for a deaf person, would be given by someone with very restricted signing skills. Never made much sense to both parents.

On both occasions, Angela refused to establish eye contact with the young woman. She would at times move about the living room or even leave the area. But their daughter did cooperate and respond fairly well, when Amy was assisting her sister during some tasks. The cooperation came because younger sis would imitate her big sis. Through both sessions, the three of them all tried to encourage Angela by giving her lots of praise.

Through those tests, it was evident that nine year old Angela was functioning at a level of three to four years old; on measures of academic aptitude (intelligence) and achievement. The aptitude testing compared her to non-handicapped children with test modifications. She had obtained higher age scores on some of the tasks when dealing with visual matching, and with language development, was considered average for a non-handicapped child of and age one and one-half year to two years old, along with some other tasks modifications.

Because of her multiple disabilities and her resistance at times to cooperate, these test results were not accurate and inconclusive. When they compared all of Angela's test results, they thought she did better on concrete and practical tasks, by using materials and situations that were more familiar to her only through continual drilling and repetition. They also stated that she wasn't flexible in applying skills to new and unfamiliar tasks. The child would also get very upset when tasks were changed.

They also had difficulty drawing conclusions on Angela's level of daily living skills, because behavior ratings by the parents and along with her teachers had showed some inconsistency. So they concluded with a possibility that Angela showed different behaviors at home than at school. Although their daughter at times will not always be compliant and will manipulate situations to get attention at home and at school, the parents had always felt that Angie definitely had the capability of learning.

✳✳✳

1984 - 1985 School Year

The summer of 1984, Frank and Dianna noticed that Angela's behavior began to deteriorate even more, with her self-abuse that was intensifying along with her frustrations. Their daughter would become angry over very simple things or things that were unaware by the other family members causing intense outbursts. She was not accepting and responding to the sign word, "No". The new outbursts included stomping loud and heavily, banging her head more upon or against objects, swinging the arms and scraping her fingernails across objects.

Mom began to leave pencils and crayons along with paper throughout different areas in their home. Sometimes when Angela became angry, she would use these items and scribble very hard on the paper sometimes causing tear. Although mom found out that the scribbling with such a degree of intensity began to heighten her frustrations even more.

Mom discovered that giving her daughter a pillow to pound into helped or something else like a stuffed teddy bear to shake or pound upon the floor. She thought that maybe it was better and safer for her daughter to vent her anger and frustrations into a pillow or any soft object.

At the end of July, Angela took the notion to simply stop and refused to walk normally. Instead of walking correctly on feet, she would walk on the toes, even hop, gallop or walk but in a very stooped position, with legs and back bent. Sometimes refusal to stand at all and she would fall down hard on her knees and move around that way.

Not understanding the reason or reasons behind the not wanting to walk upright, the mother again thought maybe something could be medically wrong. So, mom took her daughter to see the specialist once again. He examined his patient and taught the mother some therapy to perform on the child's feet and legs. The doctor disclosed that perhaps the cords in the legs were not stretching. So for several months and at least twice a day, these exercises were performed and executed.

But with each passing month Angela's rejecting to walk increased making the family to feel so perplexed about this particular problem, especially because she had always in the past once learned how to walked very well. Also, the self-abuse behavior, such as biting of the hands, sometimes until they bled and with the continual head banging had also intensified with each passing month, carrying over into another new school year.

September

Angela returned to her former public elementary school for the 1984 and 1985 school year. Her classroom was on the second floor of the building in a multi-handicap class. She started out the year fairly well and the teacher noticed that she had a desire or need for learning. Perhaps her student was beginning to come out of her shell once again.

Although Angela was nine and one-half years old and the school system knew that the parents had been communicating with their daughter at home through sign language, the system now thought it was time to push the commutative sign language skills even more. Now they realized the importance of communication!

In the past, except for one very extraordinary and caring teacher, the parents had always pushed for communication. But for some unknown reason the school system was more interested with fine and large motor skills, teaching very little commutative skills. So the first few months of school, Angela was matching more pictures with words and was signing more in the class room as well as at home.

But the little girl's behavioral problems were increasing and beginning to get in the way of her learning at school. Her teacher once again began to see a rapid deterioration beginning around the later month of November.

Angela started to exhibit a large amount of self-destructive behavior with hand biting and head banging. Her behavior had deteriorated to the point in school where it was disrupting the class and frightening the other children. For the first time the parent's daughter had begun to become physically aggressive toward the mother. In the way of shoving or pushing the mom out of her way and also striking out to hit. Once the mother had to restrain her youngest to prevent any harm to her daughter or herself. One time when restraining Angela on the dining room floor, she had bit her mother's knee and left some swelling with a very bad bruise. Mother's restraining hold on the daughter slipped which cause the incident.

Dad on several occasions had to physically hold his daughter down to keep her safe from self-abusive behaviors or from physically hurting his wife. Once Frank was restraining Angela on the kitchen floor and his parents had come in for a visit. The stunned and concerned look on their faces along with tears in their eyes, made the family feel heavy-hearted for them to see their granddaughter being restrained in that manner. Nana and Papa left the room and gave some much, needed privacy, so their son could get the granddaughter under control. Once she stopped trying to abuse herself, the resistance to fight off her dad and the sounds of her wretched crying ceased; only then was Frank able to release his hold on his tired, angry and perhaps even feeling humiliated daughter.

Later the son and his wife apologized to the parents for exposing them to a very shocking, awkward and painful incident. It wasn't easy to explain the necessity and method of restraint. But they were all too aware and sympathetic toward the problems and situations happening within their son's family life, where the granddaughter was concerned.

Although dad and mom both tried very hard to use a variety of distractions and alternative methods in the quest to help their daughter to channel the anger and abusive periods. But daily moments or periods trying to attain tolerance was becoming so short. The daughter would have an outburst while simply sitting in a rocking chair, which happen to be one of her favorite things to do.

The sign words, "No" and "Stop" was not effective any longer. So the parents tried confining her to the bedroom for ten to fifteen minutes or longer if needed; a cooling off time for their daughter to get herself under control. Numerous times she would simply refuse to submit to this and she would slam the door repeatedly, causing splintering and braking to the doorjamb. The family members had to be very careful by a door when

Angela got really agitated. One did not want to be between her and the door. Another time she used her fist so hard on the bedroom wall. Angela pounded a hole through one-half inch of plaster and several wood laths. Another outburst when she used the foot to kick up against the bedroom wall leaving a six-inch hole in diameter. Through all this the child did not harm herself.

Because of the lack of resources and all of the family's frustrations beginning to mount, spanking began by the parents, which had no effect at all on their daughter. So that form of discipline was stopped. Frank said, "I feel like I was becoming abusive myself to my little girl. The spanking was not helping the situations. I felt weak and out of control. I began to feel helpless, scared and emotionally drained." Mom hated the scenes because it caused great emotional pain, stress on Frank and more turmoil on Angela, which left her even more agitated.

Poor Amy in her young age seeing, witnessing and living the nightmare did not help her performance in schoolwork, having problems with so-called friends, or sometimes the attitude at home. Her only outlet was talking to friends that she knew could be supportive. It also affected the married couple with parenting, work related, great stress mentally and physically. The mother's was suffering and she was heading into a nervous break down and into a third spinal surgery. It was affecting the marital relationship and intimacy. Above all and the most important to get them through life's tragedies was their faith.

It was becoming increasingly apparent that Angela's inabilities to communicate, the growing behavioral problems caused by frustration was extremely overwhelming tolerance level at home and in school. The toll was taking an affect on everyone. Necessary steps were taken for the family. The young daughter was referred to a psychiatric hospital with the help from her physician and teacher because of the rapid deterioration of her behaviors.

***

January II, 1985 - February II, 1985, admitting diagnosis: Atypical pervasive developmental disorder

Principal diagnosis: A typical pervasive developmental disorder, coloboma of the left eye, with autistic features. Seizures disorder, bronchial asthma, multiple developmental delays, mental retardation, cerebellar cyst, neurogenic bladder, grossly impaired

Testing procedures done on Angela were as follows: pediatric neurology with arrangements made for examinations under anesthesia including a brain stem auditory evoked response study, electroencephalogram, CT scan. Speech therapy, occupational therapy, recreational therapy, and dentistry would be provided.

Nine-year-old mental status examinations on patient - behavior similar to a two-year-old child having tantrums. She was found to be extremely impulsive, deaf and very difficult to communicate with but at times surprisingly cooperative. Self-help skills, good with her daily living skills, limited attention span to stack four blocks with repetitive directions, excludes others by ignoring and pushing them away if physically contacted.

Electroencephalography - A painless procedure for recording electrical impulses of the brain. A variety of patterns normally produced by nerve cells are altered in recognizable ways by abnormal conditions such as epilepsy. Electroencephalography is done on a patient by placing metal plates called electrodes on the head. The electrodes are attached to a recording device that reproduces the activity graphically. The recording is called an electroencephalogram (EEG).

Brain stem or work up study on Angela, that they were able to prove that her ears were nonfunctional for hearing. A profound hearing deficit, unlikely any hearing even with aid of amplification.

During the one-month hospital stay at the medical center, Angela was seen by several specialists, such as an occupational, recreational, psychological, hearing and language therapist. They reported her attention spans would last only fifteen minutes or less and found her to be difficult, but a willingness to cooperate sometimes. Though she still continued her classes at the public school with the hospital providing the daily transportation needs.

Some psychological testing was done on the patient even though some were difficult because of her deafness. It was reported that Angela had skill ranges from ages two years to three-month level for communication. Up to four years to six months with some gross motor skills. They also reported that her level of skill was matchless with her size and her readiness. The doctors also stated that the parent's ratings were more matched with the psychological testing at the hospital than the school ratings. They felt she was being underrated for her abilities to perform in a classroom.

In summary, the daughter's extent and complexity of her problems made adequate management and other services very difficult to find in the never- ending quest for support for the family as a whole. Not only all the other existing problems but now Angela was diagnosed with having autistic tendencies. Such as rocking, extremely low tolerance of change in her environment, withdrawal from physical touch, tunes into stimulating herself with autistic-like behaviors of flapping her hands and hitting her head. Also, they felt that their patient's communication skills were very poor, even for someone who was deaf. But through all her difficulties the medical staff discovered Angela displaying affections and seeking affection out of others.

During the one-month long stay at the physiatrist hospital, on the unit, Angie had been challenged; but they told the family that she was also a delight to their nursing staff. Because most of the staff did not know sign language, Frank and Dianna made a tape of the basic signs that their daughter knew. Through that the staff blended them into her daily activities. The parents felt that the staff worked very well with Angela and they were very grateful for their nursing care towards their daughter.

Frank, Dianna and Amy were also seen by a social worker in order to help them as parents and sibling to understand and cope with their own anxieties, fears and frustrations of Angela's many difficulties in life. They were told that the three of them were doing a marvelous job in working and caring for her.

Some suggestions of techniques that both the family and the school to incorporate were: to brace up visual stimulation, practicing feelings of molding by using signs and drawings, using pencil with paper to improve her fine motor movements, encourage finger painting and practice movements in her hands by using things such as paper dolls, color forms, flannel boards and playing with dolls. As Angela got older her play interest turned to Barbie dolls and other small baby dolls and a rag doll as Raggedy Ann. Even in the future she would still enjoy playing with those dolls and dressing them especially concentrating on socks and shoes.

The family and school were instructed to continue with the behavioral therapy designed to extinguish Angela's self-destructive behaviors. A very important and value suggestion that was given to the parent's was not to incorporate negative reinforcements such as spanking. They were given other information for respite services and perhaps additional support from the Autistic Society; but the parents were put on a long waiting list for respite care.

Angela was to be followed up by one of the psychiatric doctor's with prescribed medications. Although their daughter's improvements were minimal during her long one-month stay, her self-destructive behaviors were decreased. Some time later she was prescribed a low usage of Melaril (antipsychotic) at home to help with her behavior problems.

After Angela's month's stay was finished at the hospital, she returned home very docile and non-responsive with no interaction with anyone within our family. For at least three weeks she just simply sat in a chair, with only a blank stare; and at times stay alone in her bedroom. At this time Frank and Dianna requested from the doctor to take Angie off all of her medications. For her parents felt that the medications were making their daughter a "zombie." So the psychiatric physician prescribed for her even a lower dosage of the Melaril.

During the next four weeks, the family tried several different ways to encourage interaction with Angie, in order to draw her out of the zombie-like state. First, they tried using her chalkboard that she used to print her numbers on, the alphabet and certain sign words. She would recognize and sign when those words were printed on the chalkboard. The family also tried using her flash cards and Amy's favorite rag dolls, "Raggedy Ann and Andy." But these things did not interest her at all.

Finally, dad purchased some different colored balloons and together the family started tapping the balloons across the living room between the three of them. At times they tried to include Angie and tap the balloon towards her, but at first she just simply sat and refused to participate in the game and ignored all the colorful activity around her. Perseverance prevailed until finally Angela joined in with the family!

Dad, Amy and mom watched the slow process of Angela overlooking the floating balloons, to hitting it with little emotions, like a machine robotically. Finally to where she was taking part in watching the array of rounded shaped colors being tapped gently across the living room from one concerned and happy player to the other.

Later on dad bought Angie a bright blue ball with purple dots and encourage her to roll it. At first she would just sit there on the floor with no response or interest to play yet another game. Dad also had to move her legs apart in order to roll the ball toward her. Slowly using her hands to push the ball back in the opposite direction across the floor to a different player. The family game continued until gradually Angela like a butterfly escaped from her cocoon, began to roll, throw and bounce the ball with enthusiasm. The delightful sound of giggling once again returned to her sister and parents.

For the family it had been an over whelming, frightening and unsure time in life. But a precious and blessed reward, almost like a miracle from above, One, Who had been there all the time watching, listening and guiding. Frank, Amy and Dianna had worked together striving and achieving a goal, to bring someone very close and special back and out from an automotive state.

But than more misfortune fell again upon Angela. On March 15, of 1985, mom received a phone call while at work from the school office informing her to come immediately and pick up Angela from school because of disorderly conduct. The mother received permission and left work. She drove across town with many concerns and a question forming inside her head. What happened?

When mom finally arrived at the school's office, she found her daughter sitting on a chair in a corner of the room. What mom encountered upon entering was seeing her disabled and deaf child sitting there with the look of confusion written all over her face. Looking bewildered with the lack of understanding as to "Why?" she was even sitting in a corner facing the wall. Angela's mother stopped and looked at her daughter with a teary smile. Than she signed to Angie, "Mom here now, O.K., I love you."

The principal was notified of Angela's arrival of her mother. He led mom into another room while not saying a word. He stated that Angela's outburst in the classroom was kicking off one of her shoes into the air and also knocking over a chair. Because of this incident, Angela would be suspended for five school days beginning on March 18, and she would not be allowed to return until the following week of the 25th. He also informed the mother that on the same day, her parents would had to attend a 10:00 A.M. hearing with the public school's disciplinary officer at a nearby high school skill center.

The one thing that mom really remembered before leaving the school with her daughter was how angry, feeling outraged and saying a few words back to the principal. Mom told him how she felt about the school. How that particular public school wasn't equipped or capable of handling disabled children. After all, having a handicapped class located on the second floor! Stairs! No other means to get to the classroom! For she also inquired to whether or not he had any disabled children of his own. Mom's response to his answer was, "Sir, thank God, you have healthy children, because you have no idea what it's like to raise a special child. My daughter is a handicapped child, with numerous problems, and right now is sitting on a chair in a corner, and she probably doesn't even have the knowledge or understanding, "Why?" With that statement, Angela's mother turned away from him and walked back into the office to gather her daughter for home.

The week Angela wasn't allowed back in school was very hard for her and the rest of the family. It effected all to some degree such as, Angie not accepting and understanding "Why?" she couldn't go to school. Amy's dealing with her sister's problems that resulted in her changed attitude towards her friends and her schoolwork. Pressures and stress lay very heavy upon Frank and Dianna's work performance, trying not to let the home situation jeopardize their jobs. Plus asking for help from the grandparents and other family members to care for Angela during the day.

A very good friend at work was a great help to Dianna. Not only was she supportive and a good listener, she also a mother of a deaf son. Many times Anne would share with Dianna her concerns, fears, hopes and dreams for her son; and because of her love and knowledge, guided and directed Dianna to seek legal help for Angela.

Angela's mother had contacted a gentleman from Advocates for Basic Legal Equality (ABLE). Being an advocate to help others, for he understood and cared because he himself had a disabled child of his own. So, on March 25, the parents met with their advocate, the public school hearing officer, the teacher, aid and the school principal.

Before the meeting the advocate informed the parents of their rights and told them to take along a tape recorder. He would also record the meeting for his own benefit on Angela's case. The outcome of the meeting was that Angie would be allowed to return and continue her education at school. But, Frank and Dianna, as parents were left with the feeling that the school system was on the verge of abandonment to help their daughter.

Angela's behavior problems were becoming more deteriorating with each passing day. It was getting much harder for mom to get her daughter up in the mornings and ready for school on time without her becoming combative. Sometimes the bus driver had to wait patiently for Angela because she refused to move or even walk outside onto the bus. And with mom's back problems, she wasn't able to physically pick her daughter up and carry and placed on or off the bus.

There were times when traffic was held up in front of the house, causing not only the driver of the waiting vehicles to be upset and impatient, but the bus aide as well because of the uncaring and impatient drivers. The bus driver and aid were patient and understanding. However, there were a few occasions that a bus aide became very rude toward mom about her daughter's tardiness boarding the bus. On one occasion an aide told mother to have her daughter ready, waiting and standing on the curb! Mom's retort was, "I'm sorry, but if you can't see that I am having problems just getting my daughter out the front door. I try not to hold up this bus and the traffic. But I will not allow my little girl to stand and wait for the school bus on this curb! She was taught never to go near the curb or the street, because of her being deaf."

During the week when Dianna was at work, Amy would rush home from school to meet Angie's bus. Amy too experienced times when she had problems with her sister getting her off the bus and into the house. Angela would plop her little self right down on the sidewalk and refuse to move no matter what the weather, sunny or pouring down rain, warm or cold. Sometimes Amy would struggle with her sister to get her in the house; and sometimes she would just simply walk away and let her come in on her own. But Amy would never really be too far away from her little sister.

Yes, the parents were faced with fear that the school system was dumping the whole situation onto them. And without giving the parents any help, solutions or support. Their destination with daughter Angela was growing more uncertain and the family once again faced with the unknown.

***

Wednesday, March 27, 1985

Once again while mom was at work, the school called and told her to pick Angela up and take her home. Just two days later from returning back to class, her daughter was sitting in the school's office again.

This time according to the principal and by the direction of the superintendent, Angela was removed from school on that day, because she allegedly violated the student discipline code that prohibited physical assault. Angela had bit her teacher on the thumb during the statewide tornado drill.

It had been determined Angela's presence posed a continuing danger to others, property and disrupting the academic procedures either within a classroom or elsewhere on the school's premises. During the period of removal, once again, Angie had to remain at home, not visit the school or participate in any school activities.

The parents as Angela legal guardians were advised because of the assault on the teacher, the superintendent was going to expel her for the remaining of the current semester, the rest of the school year. The parents had the opportunity to challenge the school's reason for her expulsion. Frank and Dianna were allowed the right to have a representative of their choice on Angela's behalf. Their representative also had the right to offer evidence and to question any witnesses at the hearing. The hearing was scheduled for a Friday, at 1:00 P.M., on March 29, of 1985, at the Pupil Personnel Center, headed by the hearing officer and superintendent of the public schools.

So once again, the parents took time off from work along with their advocate from ABLE to attend the hearing. At this meeting everyone learned that the teacher had taken her classroom down to the school's basement fifteen minutes prior to the tornado drill. After the tornado bell sounded, the hallway started to fill up with the school's students.

Their daughter became agitated, while sitting on the floor and started to bite her hands. Her teacher grabbed and pulled Angela's hands out of her mouth, which caused her student to become even more agitated. So she continued to bite at her hands. When Angela's teacher attempted again to stop her from biting her hands, Angela bit her. Because of this action, she would be expelled from school permanently.

The public school superintendent offered for Angela home instructions for one hour a week. Frank and Dianna fought this decision because they wanted their daughter's education held within school surroundings, along with other children. But instead the best the parents could get for their little girl was three times a week, one-hour sessions after school hours and just with her teacher only.

Mom and dad insisted that a school bus and not a cab would pick their daughter up from home to school in order to keep somewhat of a normalcy within her life. Besides the parents felt that the biting incident was accidentally done on Angela's part because at the hearing the teacher did admit that her hands could have been in the wrong spot during re-straining.

Before leaving the meeting, Frank and Dianna had to sign a place-ment form for Angela. This form stated because of the student's extent of disabilities, "No" supplemental services, "No" individual/small group in-struction, "No" learning center in a public school building in the district and "No" other learning center in another district. "Yes" to a learning center in a separate facility and "Yes" to home instructions for the dura-tion period of the school year. The parents signed this form but after their signatures they wrote, "Parents disagree with this placement."

Because Angela's parents protested against the expulsion from school and the limited amount of education offered, their advocate suggested to them to get an attorney. His impressions were that they needed more legal advice regarding the daughter's rights and she was definitely not getting a fare shake from the public school's decision.

An appointment was arranged by their advocate and they were intro-duced to a gentleman who was a full time attorney within ABLE. By the time the parents met with the other gentleman, he had already read the full report on Angela's case. After filling in a few more questions with answers from mom and dad, the attorney agreed to take their daughter's case. He appeared to them as a man with knowledge on "Rights for the Disable." His sympathetic attitude and concern had given Angela's parents some hope that their daughter would be considered as a person with rights and feelings.

In the meantime the whole family life was indeed disrupted. Dad and mom were missing work because of meetings and of course Angela's care during the day. Her daily schedule or routine was torn completely apart and for an autistic-like child this presented more problems for the family in controlling her behavior. The stress and tension within the home life was once again affecting Amy's attitude and schoolwork. She was quiet, moody, cocky and defensive. Sure thing these were signs of feelings of neglect. Mom and dad tried to keep communication lines open with the oldest daughter, dad more than mom was there for Amy.

Once again because of mom's job, she had to depend on her own mother, her sister Deb and her husband's sister Betty to help out with Angela's daily care. Nana helped whenever she could because of her work-ing during the day. Through all of this another meeting was scheduled to discuss the rights on her education, giving only seven hours per week and still the questions with the transportation.

Before the next encounter, the parents had some concerns and information about the daughter's behavior for their attorney. Such as: Angela's routine was affecting her behavior during the day and she was up throughout the nighttime. They also had questions and demands for the school board such as:

1. What type of transportation to school?

2. If taxi must have an aide?

3. Would transportation be provided so that Angela could continue her weekly after school special program sessions?

4. Why is only seven hours per week?

5. Why not nine hours per week? Seven hours was only 22% of her regular school hours!

6. No more work to be missed by parents, set up evening meeting on April 19, at 5:00 P.M.

7. Parents wish to observe all classes without disturbing the environment of class routine.

8. When exactly will classes begin? Since the school had drastically cut the school hours for her, they wanted every minute for her accounted for Angela during the class time.

9. How do you justify cutting her school hours, will help the behaviors or her learning abilities from all her reports given through the psychiatric hospital?

10. What are you prepared to do if this causes a worse behavioral condition before the April 19, meeting?

On April 19, the parents met again with the public school chairperson, assistant superintendent, the attorney for the parents representing Angela and a principal from a special disabled school and others again. The new gentleman represented a school that provided education for special children with various degrees of mental retardation, behavior or other disabilities. Their special resources and dedication would provide education in hopes to mainstream these special children back into the school system. He had sat in on the meeting and would review Angela's case.

Angela's final Individualized Education Program occurred on April 24, of 1985. The public school system agreed to provide the program for Developmentally Handicapped and related services with seven hours per week of transportation, occupational therapy and language development beginning in April of 1985 and continuing until June of 1985. Angela would participate with non-handicap students in the classroom. An Individualized Education Program for short and annual goal was:

Short-term instructional objectives:

1. Name consonants and vowels when shown letter

2. Read simple words when paired with pictures

3   Read by sight ten words without picture

    Annual goal: To improve math skills
    Short Term instructional objectives:

1. Construct sets of one to five objects

2. Read (sign) numbers one to ten

3. Match sets one to ten with appropriate number

4. Begin number writing

    Annual goal: To improve social skills
    Behavioral management program will be used
    Short-term instructional objectives:

1. Sit upright position when working at table

2. Stand and walk in upright position without command

    Annual goal: Occupational therapy will be provided two and one-half sessions per week
    Annual goal: To improve language skills

1. Spontaneously name the familiar objects

2. Produce signs for classmates when shown card (what classmates?)

3.   3. Sign her needs 75% of the time

4. Sign 25 words without pictures

Also an appointment was arranged for Angela and her parents to visit with the principal and some staff of this new school for the coming fall school year 1985 - 1986.

When the meeting adjourned Frank and Dianna along with the principal of the new school for the disabled and the attorney stepped out into the hall. The parents expressed their deepest appreciation and thankfulness to the principal. They declared their hopes and feelings for Angela's acceptance for her new school placement in the coming up fall. Together, mom and dad enunciated their anxieties, the setbacks with an emotionless interest in regards to the next meeting of touring his school. Before he departed from the parents shook hands in acceptance.

Angela's parents then turned their attentions back to their attorney and continued conversing about the outcome of the events. As the three of them stood there in the hall, Frank had noticed the assistant superintendent walked by them and disappeared into an office behind the small group. Just as the three of them had finished with the conversation, the gentleman exited from the room and proceeded to approach the parents as he headed for the stairway.

He came up along the side of Angela's dad and made eye contact with him and extended his hand and said, " If there is anything I can do please let me know." Frank stopped and looked straight at the gentleman with his hand down along the side of his leg and retorted back, "I think you have done enough already." With that remark from Angela's father, he then turned and continued down the stairway.

Now when the parents think back to that particular, copious school year of 1985, they feel the only people that had shown concern about Angela's feelings and welfare were her family, other family members and close friends. And of course the three gentlemen that came into our lives, the advocate from ABLE, the attorney from there and the principal who worked at a special handicap school for the disabled children.

Once again God had listened to the prayers of the family and blessed them with good, concern, caring and understanding people to be in their life. Perhaps later the family would be able to hear reports from new teachers about a happy and giggling student.

PART 4

And the building blocks came tumbling down...

The summer of 1985 and throughout Angela's first year starting at the new school was extremely difficult for her and the worst time ever for the entire family. Her mental and physical deteriorations were progressing more rapidly for her, becoming more noticeable by family, friends and school authority; more harder to deal and cope with for everyone concerned.

Little did Frank and Dianna realized or even wanted to admit that they were reaching the peak of their long and laboring mountainous struggle with their daughter. They were about to descend or tumble down the other side into what or where? Dared not even think about what the next plateau on that tumultuous mountain would bring. Little did the two of them actually know that within that year of the downfall, the parents would finally reach a sad period together in the form of a realistic judgment that led to a heart-breaking decision?

For all too soon the dawn of realization came upon the couple when the two of them silently admitted to themselves, that their daughter's problems were growing beyond their control. But it would take another long year of several disheartening incidents before husband and wife could have the courage and strength to voice their feelings to one another without the fear of hurting each other.

The family life had become nothing more than a constant daily struggle to maintain everything each one of them had worked so hard to achieve and sacrificed for; just to hold onto the tiniest bit of normalcy of life style within the family. For Angela, a young girl trying to grow up normally but is dealt a hand that deals with a difficult and mental challenge. For Amy so young and impressible, to live with a stressful situation in the home and trying to be herself, or at school and even around her friends. For some of her close friends knew what was happening and taking place within the home. Whether they heard first hand from Amy or witness the circumstances when staying over or spending time at the house. The husband trying to be both spouse and father going to work daily but the constant and nagging thoughts how his family was living a stressful and very intense life. The wife trying to be both spouse and mother living daily with constant and nagging thoughts of her own and how her family was living in a very intense and stressful life.

Never really knowing how each day was to begin or end, if she was doing the right things for all concern, trying to give quality time and care for all but knowing that her husband and the older daughter was being cheated from her because most of her time went to the youngest. The continual feelings of guilt laying so heavy upon her shoulders, feeling like she was so alone.

Feeling so alone... Angela living in a silent world, confused world, unknown world...a life of being loved but existing in a crazy, turbulent, emotional and physical imbalance existence.

Since Angela had always needed constant supervision and even more so in the summer months of no school, Dianna requested and fortunately got summers off from her job, thanks to an understanding employer. This didn't help their financial situation at home, but it did ease the constant problem of arranging dependable in-home care for the girls, especially with Angela's situation.

The majority of the time, it had usually been the couple's parents, Dianna's sister or Frank's sister. And as Angela's problems worsened, the parents found that family were the only ones they could trust and depend on. Angela's parents tried not to take advantage of their family's willingness to help. They only called on them for emergency situations or if they felt desperately needed a brake from the around-the-clock care. But the time away from the children or situations were limited and short.

When Angela's condition worsened, the family could see the burden it was taking on Frank, Amy and Dianna. Perhaps an even terrible thought was the toll that was taking place on Angela. So the loving and caring family members were coming over to the house more often to give help, advice, comfort and support.

At that point in time though, the weary family only social outlet was being involved with Amy and her school activities. Frank most of the time would try to attend games or functions by himself because it had become so impossible to take Angela anywhere, for she was regressing more and more everyday. She refused to walk correctly, preferring only to walk on her knees. If anyone tried to enforce her to walk upright, she would just simply jump down on her knees all the harder, becoming and showing much anger.

Anger with pulling at her hair, ripping and tearing her clothing, smacking herself in the face, head banging and biting at her hands, arms and legs leaving bite marks and bruises. Sometimes the anger would lead to striking out at family members mostly her mother. There were times she would head bang on walls and floors or hit, strike, punch with hands on windows, walls and anything else or anyone in her way.

Angela could and would ignore others and wanted to be left alone. Even though there were some rare times that she like attention and love shown to her, but there were those moments when she didn't want to be touched or have any bodily contact, such as hugs, a gentle touch, pat upon her hand, arm or on her cheek. Kisses, she always enjoyed giving or receiving those, but even a kiss was becoming rare, just like the sounds of her happy and giggling self.

There were less giggles and more sounds of anger and frustration. With every passing day, Angela was slowly regressing into a reclusive state. Once again, she was slipping away from everyone and everything, sliding swiftly into her own little, silent and quiet world that she lived and experienced. But the world she knew was spinning out of control, a shattered, raging, trouble and painful world that her family found themselves this time unable to enter and rescue their precious one from.

The daughter, the sister was getting upset more easier and would show her frustrations by stomping throughout the house, banging doors until the plaster fell or the door jambs would brake from the force of slamming the doors. Once she almost slammed the bedroom door on her mother's hand. The daughter was becoming more abusive towards mom by striking out and hitting at her. Mother had to be more cautious when climbing and descending the stairs with Angela, positioning herself either in front or behind her daughter. For there were times when Angela turned on her mother and tried to push mom down the steps.

Angela's other self-abusive behaviors increased such as biting of her hands which now had raised scar tissue areas on them. She also bit her arms and legs leaving severe bite marks and bruises. Also the continual slapping to her eyes and face. She completely stopped eating with her utensils and would eat with her fingers. Mother had to put away all the glasses for drinking and buy plastic because the daughter would bite down so hard while drinking, causing pieces of glass to brake off into her mouth.

Some of her autistic tendencies were becoming more visible again. For example, Angela would stare at herself in the mirror, spinning dishes and various objects. Her fatuous with shoes increased for herself and on others, constant rocking and her inability to cope with any changes. Sometimes mom cleaned the house and would move the furniture around in the living room or bedrooms. Not knowing or really understanding that those changes would cause her daughter to get upset. Also any changes in the regular routine of school or within the home.

At bedtime Angela would get so upset and tore her whole bed apart. Throwing the sheets, protective padding, blankets and mattress about the room. Once the bed was remade, Angela finally being somewhat calm and lying down, mom thought the night would bring her daughter rest and sleep. And lo and behold, now her daughter was staying up through the night without much rest. Angela also started with having urinary and bowel control problems once again. Almost every night mom could be found stripping her bedding, cleaning up her accidents in the bedroom, hallway and into the bathroom.

Frank would sleep right through those nightly incidents and his wife tried not to disturb him or Amy, because both had to get up early for work and school. Although wife and mother after a long period of time dealing with this nightly regiment was becoming very exhausted from everything. Depression was taking its hold on Dianna. Than in April of 1989 an accident at her job landed her with a fourth back surgery and fusion. Not only emotionally but physically as well.

Dianna had no life or time for herself. She felt like a zombie, programmed only for the sole responsibility and care of her daughter. Mother had little or no time for Frank and Amy. With everything happening between the spouses there was a lot of stress and strain upon their marital relationship. They had no time for intimacy because Dianna was always so exhausted and Frank was avoiding the home situation by working day and night. Amy was suffering silently too. Realizing her mother was too busy with her sister, Amy turned to a couple of close school friends.

To confide in with sharing the family secrets, living the unknown and stressful incidents taking place at home concerning her sister's emotional and physical traumas and problems. Perhaps even conversations about the neglect that she was feeling at home from her own parents, who were just too busy with work or overwhelmed with her sister's concerns. Justified, truly for the way she felt, Amy indeed had every right to feel the justification in the way her life was going by sharing the uncontrolled problems, concerns and stress that was taking over her family's life.

At Angela's new school the behavior problems had gotten in the way of her education. The school's first intention was to get some control over Angela, even before instruction of educating her could begin. Behaviors were definitely getting in the way of education. The school did succeed to a small degree in controlling Angela's behavior, thus allowing them to achieve some educational goals. At least they, everyone in the school that knew her and wanted to help, were able to get her off her knees and back to walking correctly.

So many of the school's employees gave their time, concern, help and love to a very special student. Someone who later would give in return her special ways of gratitude and love. Later on the parents and their older daughter would be so grateful and blessed for all those who gave of themselves.

Dianna returned to work in the fall of 1985. In order to be ready for her job on time, she would have to rise at 4:30 A.M. and get ready before anyone else in the household. She would then prepare the family's breakfast and school lunches, if not prepared the night before for Amy and Angela. Then Dianna got Frank up at 5:45 A.M. for work, Amy up at 6:30 A.M. for school and finally Angie at 7:00 A.M. for bus and school.

Mother dreaded getting up during the week for school mornings and facing her youngest combative disposition. It was a constant battle each morning just to get her daughter out of bed, bathed if there was a voiding accident during the night, the forever and repetitive signing, praying and retrieving the tossed and thrown away clothing. After the struggle of dressing, was the breakfast which usually went smoothly, but the only problem was that she ate extremely slow, so if one tried to hasten her, look out because all hell would brake loose!

Once breakfast was accomplished then the brushing of the teeth, hair and other little minor things. When child, coat and etc. with school bag at hand, the wait at the front door, on the porch or outside depending on the weather for the school bus. But if the bus was late, heaven and God help us all! Angela would run and stomp through the house banging her hands on the walls, doors, windows and mirrors.

Sometimes she would even tear at her clothing, slapping her face, biting at herself and pulling out strands of her own hair. The child would make some sad and low vocal, whimpering sounds like a wounded or trapped animal.

Dianna found herself constantly planning, timing and orchestrating ways to eliminate and deal with Angela's angry and frustrating mornings. But no matter how hard mom tried, nothing seem to work, in fact by altering things around only made some mornings worse than others. So no matter what the outcome was going to turn out for both, mom and daughter, the goal was get Angela ready and organized for the bus.

She always took to school a notebook for communication between parent and teachers. Always to inform how the evenings before and mornings prior before school. The instructors wrote back to share how Angela's day went. And once mom's little girl was finally on the bus and enrouted to school, mother would feel so alone, frightened and exhausted that usually for several minutes she would just sit there in that empty house crying; calling on God for help and asking Him why? Why? Then she would recompose herself and leave for work.

There were several mornings though, Dianna felt terribly stressed and exhausted that she would sometimes phone her mother or her sisters just to talk about the morning and receive advice, comfort and support before reporting to work. One morning in particular, Dianna never made it to her job. Angela was extremely difficult to handle, like another unknown person, possessed and completely out of control. And mom facing a battle she could not win.

Angela had gotten up much more combative and angrier, than mom had ever seen. Her daughter was more adamant than ever before about not wanting to take her morning bath or even wash up some because she smelled like urine from another voiding accident.

She started crying in that high pitch whining tone of hers, tearing at her night clothing and slamming the walls with her hands. Mother had wrestled and fought with her to get the wet and smelly clothing off of her. Mom knowing the time tried hard not to be impatient as she sign and gave aid to the washing and signing again so as not to abuse herself.

But Angela's mental state exploded and mother felt like she had drowned. Her daughter's hands were bleeding from her biting and Dianna was losing both ground and patience in the battle to finish the bath and get her dressed for school.

Dianna was having difficulty in restraining Angela during her episodes, because her daughter had become heavier and much more stronger. Also her mother's back problems and recent surgeries had made it more difficult for mom to physically restrain because Angela would overpower her mother.

Somehow mother and daughter finished the dressing and descended down the stairs to the kitchen. Amy had already left for school with her friends. Once downstairs Angela quieted down long enough to eat her breakfast. But once she was finished, all hell had broken loose. Like the person possessed, a demonic maniac, bent on self-destruction. She ran through the house slamming her hands against the walls, windows and doors, to such an intense degree, that mom became thoroughly frightened for her daughter's safety. And when mother tried to approach Angela to restrain her, her daughter struck out at mom hitting and hurting.

So Dianna backed off and just stood there in the living room, watching, crying and signing, as Angela slammed her hands against the glass mirror above the fireplace. Then her daughter sat down and proceeded to slam and bang her head against the brick of the fireplace, moaning and crying so forlornly.

Dianna realized that she needed some help. She had completely lost perspective and control. Shaking, she walked over to the telephone and dialed Betty's number. After a few rings that seemed an eternity for Dianna, the phone was plucked from its holder. The sound of her sister-in-law's voice told Angela's aunt everything. Being aware and knowing the circumstances in the mornings, living only a few minutes from there, Betty had walked over from hearing the urgency in the voice coming from the phone call. Together aunt and mom managed to have Angela ready and walked outside to be put on the school bus.

But mom continued to shake, felt weary and drained as the two of them slowly walked back into the house. Dianna sat down upon the sofa and just instantaneously started to cry uncontrollable. Sobbing she tried to describe to Betty the horror of that morning. How Angela had turned on her mother and how mom could not control the whole and entire situation getting someone ready for the school bus.

Betty sat quietly in the living room and listened. She tried to calm Dianna down, but to no avail. Her sister-in-law complained of having chest pain, the feeling a little strange or numb feeling and also a difficult time of breathing. The very concern woman stood up and left the living room to find a brown paper bag from the kitchen drawn. She handed it to Dianna and told her to breathe into it. Betty explained that she was hyperventilating. After several minutes of watching, listening and breathing into a bag, Dianna heard the next comment.

Concerned, Betty insisted a trip to the hospital. Dianna's frightened and bewilderment expression wandered from her friend to the bag that lay on her lap. Feeling drained and exhausted from the whole episode that morning, she felt too tired to disagree or argue.

Dianna was taken to the nearest hospital being examined for hyperventilation brought on by a severe anxiety attack. While she was in the examination room, Betty was taken aside by one of the emergency's doctor's on duty for some questioning regarding her sister-in-law's condition. He wanted information about his patient that she had brought in to the hospital.

The questions directed at Betty were to find out what she knew about Dianna's life at home. What was going on to have caused such great emotional stress? Was the situation at home was the result of an abusive husband? Of course that question threw Betty a curve! She was caught off guard and a little frightened by his barrage method of interrogation.

Gathering her composure, she explained to them the true status within his patient's home regarding her niece. Upon hearing and trying to understand the whole picture of the given conversation; and learning that Dianna essentially had the full brunt of her daughter's care. The doctor then wanted to know what was being done if anything to help her in dealing with that particular situation because just by his initial observation of the emotional state she was in, the older gentleman warned Betty that her sister-in-law was most likely headed for very bad nervous breakdown.

Frank's sister further told them that the family as a whole had always been supportive and helped out as much as they possibly could; and that the family also realized that nothing more could be done until her brother and his wife accepted the truth. The truth being that Dianna alone could no longer give her daughter proper care and help that Angela desperately needed, without some form of professional intervention.

ANNIVERSARY GIFT

That necessary help first came in the form of spiritual intervention. It happened that April of 1986, during school spring break, Dianna's sister, Deb, had been coming over a few days each week to stay with the girls and help out while Dianna was at work.

One particular Friday, late afternoon when Dianna arrived home from work, she and her sister stood outside and talked for a good while. Dianna was very despondent and she found herself unburdening all her spent up feelings unto her sister. The sister stood there quietly, listening and then consoled her sibling with these words.

✲✲✲

"Di, I know you have been dealing with an awful lot all these years, both you and Frank. I understand somewhat what you must be going through as I have helped you out, but not on a twenty-four hour basis like you've been doing. God knows, I have my own problems. You and Frank have helped me out through some of those rough times. You know Di, what I am trying to say is, we all have difficulties to deal with in life or crosses to carry upon our shoulders. I know you must feel that you just can't take any more of it! But Di, somehow, you will get through this with Angela. Frank and Amy will too. I want, can I ask you a personal question?" After seeing a slight shake of her sister's head, she continued. " When was the last time you went to church? And please be honest with yourself!"

✲✲✲

Dianna was somewhat surprised by her sister's question. Feeling somewhat embarrassed, Dianna confessed, "Well Deb, to be honest with you, I really guess it's been a long time, too long of a time."

✲✲✲

"Well Di, attending church again could be your hope and answer. I found out for myself that Sunday Mass really helps me to get through another week. It gives me strength to go on when I don't feel or want to anymore. I know my problems are different compare to what all of you are experiencing and have been going through all these years. But, I truly believe this will and can very much help you. I'm going to the 11:00 A.M.

227

Mass on Sunday. Give me a call tomorrow evening if you want me to pick you up." With that, Deb gave her sister a hug and left for home.

Dianna thought about what her sister said all that evening and the following day on Saturday. She mentioned her conversation she had with her sister the day before to her husband. Frank's words of encouragement were simply stated, "Di, if that's what you want to do, than go to church with your sister. I'll stay home and not plan to work tomorrow and take care of the girls."

Being raised from a Baptist background, Frank never discouraged his wife from practicing her faith of Catholicism. Dianna had fallen away from the Church by her own choice.

Dianna picked up the telephone that laid on a table in the dining room and dialed her sister's number. Anxiously she waited until she finally heard a quiet voice pick up on the other end of the line. Deb sounded surprised or elated to here back from her sibling about her decision to attend Mass the next day. Deb told her sister to be ready at 10:30 the following morning. She was also delighted that Dianna had called. Before the line went dead, one end heard "Thanks" and the other end heard "I Love You."

One spring morning, a cloudless blue sky, the sun shining bright through the car's windshield window as it headed toward its destination of a big and beautiful old stone church. It was a Sunday morning on April 21, of 1986. Within minutes there would be two young women joining and kneeling among the congregation to celebrate Mass. Two sisters together kneeling side by side, heart felt and silently praying to God. One prayed for strength to become once more a strong woman in starting a new life and the continual role as mother for her two sons. The other sister asking for God's help for her family and especially forgiveness for her long absence away from Him.

The memory of that specific and lovely spring Sunday morning will always remain a picture in Dianna's mind and heart. First reason because on that Sunday it happened to be her fourteenth wedding anniversary. Secondly Dianna received from her sister that morning a very important message and gift. Deb's sister finally realized that one could never be possibly alone in life to carry those heavy crosses.

For He, God would always be there for her, one just have to walk into His open arms. To accept His strength, hear the words of guidance and feel His love like the warmth from the sun. Dianna's faith emerged and took form to become the most important thing in her life. Without this new inner spiritual growth, this woman probably would not have made it through the forthcoming months.

In fact by the fall of 1988, Dianna's husband's Frank had decided to join the Catholic Church. For some time he had been noticing what her faith was doing for her, and he wanted also for them to share in it together. His decision was not only based on what he was witnessing with his wife, but he too had been searching and praying to God for strength and answers.

So in the fall of 1988, Frank enrolled in the Rites of Christian Initiation of Adults Program. By the spring of 1989, at the Easter Vigil, (Holy Saturday), Frank was baptized, confirmed and received his First Communion.

***

Frank and Dianna received a letter a precious gift from his Aunt Eleanor, Papa's sister. She inquired how their family was doing. His aunt mentioned that Nana and Papa had been keeping her informed about the situation with their granddaughter Angela. She wanted everyone to know that they were always in her thoughts and prayers. Along with the aunt's letter was also enclosed a page she had found in an old prayer book.

***

Welcoming A Special Child
Whosoever shall receive one of such children in My name, received Me. (Mark, 9:37)

Although caring for a handicapped child poses many problems and can be very demanding, parents should welcome the little one into their home with thanksgiving. God richly rewards those who accept such a challenge with grace and devotion.

By Edna Massimilla has written this touching verse:
A meeting was held quite far from earth;
It's time again for another birth.
Said the angels to the Lord above,
"This special child will need much love.
He may not run or laugh or play;
His thoughts may seem quite far away.
In many ways he won't adapt,

And he'll be known as handicapped.
So let's be careful where he's sent;
We want his life to be content.
Please, Lord, find the parents who
Will do a special job for You.
They will not realize right away
The leading role they're asked to play;
But with this child sent from above
Comes stronger faith and richer love.
And soon they'll know the privilege given
In caring for their gift from heaven;
Their precious charge, so meek and mild,
Is heaven's very special child.

If God has allowed a handicapped child to come into your life, He has considered you worthy of such a trust. Receive that precious one the way our Savior welcomed the little children when He was here on earth.

-H.G.B.

Real love is helping someone for Jesus' sake
Who can never return the favor.

THE SHUNT

May 28, 1986 - June 10, 1986: admittance for vomiting, stumbling and possible headaches, shunt implant

**

Shunt (Hydrocephalus - water on the brain), a tube or shunt is surgically inserted into the head, down the side of the neck and into the lower abdomen to drain the fluid from the brain. This procedure was required in Angela's case. It was an involved surgery of total with three incisions; a C shaped hole was drilled in the skull, incision within the neck and the third one on her lower abdomen. The tube usually remains in place for life, but as the person grows, the tube may become blocked, thus allowing pressure to build up in the brain. Irritability and vomiting will occur. If this happens immediate hospitalization would be needed and the blockage removed or the tube replaced.

**

Now along with Angela's combative outbursts, there were growing moments of apathy when she would just simply sit or lay around the house. Her parents and sister started noticing that Angela was holding her head and making pathetic whimpering or whining sounds.

At the dinner table the family noticed how she would become lethargic. She would sit at the table and cradled her head with one of her hands. And on a few occasions Angela would sign to her mother, "hurt, and head." Mom and dad felt that something physically was wrong manifesting because of their daughter's high pain tolerance. It was very difficult for the parents to know when something was hurting their little girl, for it was rare when she would sign "hurt."

It was first that the parents thought it was just another phase of her emotional behavior patterns. But when Angela started to stagger as she walked and had a few bouts with vomiting, her mother suspected that something could be wrong. Even Angela's teachers at school were reporting her listlessness.

Dianna made an appointment with her daughter's doctor, for mom feared with her vomiting and staggering that something seriously had to be going on. To both dad and mom, their daughter looked as if she was suffering from severe headaches. As usual the doctor's examination and concern for his patient's well being had led the patient's parents to another appointment for a brain wave test on their daughter.

The test was scheduled at a clinic across town, along with certain instructions from the physician for Dianna to get Angela prepared and readied. Mother had to administer one-half of prescribed medication for relaxation to her daughter before they left the house for the clinic.

So the morning of the appointment both grandmothers and Frank's sister accompanied Dianna for moral support to help her with Angela. Once the five of them arrived at the clinic, a nurse gave Angela the other half of her medication. Of course the whole while the little patient kept signing "NO!" Than the group were all ushered into a waiting room to sit and wait for Angela to become relaxed and sleepy.

After thirty minutes or longer, extra medication was again prescribed and given once more. But Angela just continued to sit there in the waiting room, giggling, giggling and signing "NO SLEEP!" So the waiting four continued their vigilance and waiting, waiting and waiting. But, instead, the other four women were the ones relaxing, becoming very sleepy and laughing. While Angela on the other hand never got tired or relaxed enough for the test. So no more medication could be given to her and the test was canceled. Betty with her wry humor said, "Well, time to go home girls, the party is breaking up!"

***

The next venture in preparation for Angela's hospital admission was a trip to the outpatient unit for blood work to be drawn. Her doctor had contacted the hospital prior to his patient's arrival explaining to them about Angela's disabilities and her fears of hospitals. By now eleven-year old Angela had developed a total fear of the hospital and anyone in white. He also explained how her mother would have to be there with her daughter the whole time for communication purposes. He instructed the staff to have everything ready when they arrive with her.

Knowing what Dianna knew in the past about her daughter's fears of needles and other hospital procedures, mom voiced her concerns to the doctor. Angela's physician in return assured mother that everyone at the hospital would be more prepared to deal with Angela's reactions. He responded, "We have to try and get as much of these tests completed as an outpatient, in case she is admitted. It will decrease the amount of days she would have to stay in the hospital. I realize that this will be hard on you and Angela, but we must try."

So another appointment had to be scheduled. Dianna called Betty and asked her if she could be available to go and help out with her niece. Betty answered, "No problem."

The dreaded appointment day arrived all too soon for mom. When Dianna drove into the hospital's parking lot, she looked over at Betty in anticipation for some kind of reaction from Angela. With no outburst of any kind, Angela's aunt murmured, "So far, so good."

Angela was a little hesitant though about getting out of the car. She seemed to sense what was coming. Dianna and Betty nonchalantly walked slowly with Angela to their destination for her blood work. Mom quickly announced her daughter's name at the outpatient window and one of the nurses brought out a wheelchair. The young patient sat down but immediately jumped up from the chair and started to get upset by vocalizing very loud sounds of panic, slapping herself and biting at her hands.

Within several long minutes two lab nurses in white realized that they alone were not going to be able to draw blood from the young girl acting this way. So they informed the patient's mother that they would have to call down their "A Team." (two to four orderlies). Right away Dianna told the two nurses to stress the fact that her daughter was very frightened and upset, and for them to move slowly toward her and PLEASE have them remove their white lab jackets before they enter the room. In a matter of minutes the "A Team" arrived, entering the room with their lab coats on and started quickly right towards the already frightened patient.

How can one say it? Immediately, fear struck Angela! She jumped out of the wheelchair and ran away from the "A Team." Dianna's terrified daughter vocalizing her loud sounds of fear and ran around the room pounding on the hospital's walls. There was a bathroom off from the room where she escaped into and slammed the door on everyone! The lab nurses, the so called "A Team" and others that heard and saw the commotion all just stood looking stunned with disbelief written all over their faces.

The mother of the overpowering fear daughter looked over at the aunt and said, "I tried to warn them, I tried to tell them. What am I? I am just the mother, I don't know anything!" Dianna spoke out loud as she looked at Betty. "They had to find out for themselves. Didn't want to listen to you, they probably thought you were exaggerating. Now they saw and now they know!" Said Betty.

The "A Team" glanced over at the patient's mother and responded. "We're not touching her!" And after that comment they all left the room. Betty and Dianna stood there, collected themselves and gave Angela some time to herself to calm down. After several minutes the once terrified girl opened the door slowly and peek out at her mother at aunt.

Dianna smiled and signed to her daughter "O.K., go home now." Her daughter was very careful when opening the door wide. She still looked frightened and unsure of things around her and made some sad, loud vocal sounds. Mom tried to reassure her daughter by a smile, signing again "O.K., go home and love you."

Dianna approached Angela slowly and gently touched her daughter's cheek and gave her a hug. Aunt Betty smiled at her niece with tears in her eyes. As the three ladies slowly walked and exited the building the lab nurse picked up the phone. She called the office of Angela's doctor and informed him how the patient had frightened off their "A Team"; blood work definitely canceled!

Now there were two unsuccessful attempts of test preparations for Angela. Should the Three Musketeers try for three? One more outpatient test was scheduled at the hospital. The third was a CT scan. Once again Dianna and Betty pulled up into the hospital's outpatient parking lot. The two women held their breath and looked at each other waiting for some kind of reaction from the passenger sitting in the back seat. Mother and aunt both were thinking the same thing. Will Angela get out of the car? Will they even get her into the hospital? And how will this adventure end today?

✳✳✳

Betty said, "Di, wait here and I'll run in and get a wheel chair."

✳✳✳

Cautiously and hesitantly, Angela got out of the car and unsteadily climbed into the wheelchair. So far so good! The three started for their destination to the Radiology Department. Again so far so good! Dianna announced her daughter's name and once more the three were ushered into a waiting area. Inside the waiting room area two nurses approached slowly and carefully to the young girl sitting in the chair.

Both women seemed to be aware of the problems before and one of them explained to mother, how she and along with mom's and the aunt's help to strap Angela into the wheelchair. Than and only than could the injection could be administered to the patient. The medication would make her relax and sleepy. Of course this procedure had to go slowly and on mom's cue.

The cue was given but the four involved had struggled some during the strapping down with Angela into the wheelchair. The frightened and this time the very agitated child actually overpowered her agents and stood up, chair and all when she saw the exposed needle! Of course the subject of the needle was brought up. Please do not let Angela see it! Everyone involved were at one point afraid that someone was going to be the target! One of the nurses remarked how there was enough medication to knock out an elephant. This was mentioned as a joke to ease up some of the tension.

Finally giving up fighting against the restraining straps and her encamptors, Angela gave in and sat down unhappily in the wheelchair. For almost ninety minutes before showing any signs of drowsiness she sat restrained. Mother was asked to accompany her daughter and went with her into the X-ray room. Mom stayed with her until she was finally asleep. She was then asked to leave the room during her daughter's CT scan.

Back in the waiting room, Betty and Dianna had smelled a very strong gas-like odor. After a while the two were becoming quite anxious, bored and somewhat giddy; so the women decided to walk down the halls and just talk. Betty jokingly commented, "You know Di, from now on, when my niece sees me, she'll probably relate her Aunt Bet with doctors and hospitals."

Even though they laughed over her silly remark, both of them knew that it was really true. For Angela had an uncanny way of associating people with events in her life. She would react to those in a very negative way if the event were stressful or painful for her. Thus, Angela's fragile accomplishments of behavior control would be lost.

Dianna looked over at her sister-in-law with a smile and commented how they were making memories with Angela. Some good and fun while the other outings were those one wanted to just simply forget and wipe out from the memory part of the brain. But Dianna was always grateful for having Bet around especially times like those. She also knew that one could get very emotional, stressed and wearied.

Sometimes never really knowing how the events with Angela would turn out. Having Betty with her helped so much, for Bet, like others, always gave her strength, support and no matter how hard or difficult, she knew that Frank's sister would be there for her and her niece. There were times when one could make a joke, find humor, looked for the positive out of a negative. Especially like now when the two of them were tired from the incident, tired emotionally and even physically.

It was very hard that day for mom going through everything with her daughter. So down deep in her heart, Dianna knew that Betty was handling everything going on with her niece so well. Bet was trying to be upbeat and funny to relieve some of the stress. Earlier Dianna saw the tears in Betty eyes as she helped restrained her precious niece to the wheelchair. But in Angela's eyes, her Aunt Bet loved her and vice versa.

The two women took Angela home right after her CT scan to wait on the results. Within the next few days her condition worsened with increased vomiting and regression with her refusal to walk. She would use crab-like movements across the floor, whining and grabbing at her head.

Dianna called Angela's doctor and he suggested immediately but compassionately to the mother to admit his patient right away. The doctor knew that mom was doing and trying her damnest to be there for her daughter. Just mention another hospital admittance would cause the patient's mother to cry. Her bravery front would disappear quickly because she always knew how the hospital stays were so hard on her daughter. Emotionally draining on both mother and daughter, along with dad and older sister.

So when the neurologist read the CT scan and took one look at Angela lying pitifully on the hospital's pediatrics' playroom floor holding her head, he immediately scheduled surgery to implant a shunt to relieve the ventricle pressure of the excess fluid that was building up in her cranial cavity.

This was one of the most painful and stressful times in the family's life. One would think by now, the family would have been conditioned from Angela's numerous medical problems. The parents just wanted to get through this one more traumatic experience and put it behind them and go on with their lives, no matter what God was giving and putting upon their shoulders.

Never again to think about this painful ordeal that Angela and all of them had to undergo with the surgery and the weeks afterwards. Dianna had shoved the memories of this particular event so far back in her mind, that it is very painful for her even now to recall everything.

She and the family will always remember that Angela had very long and beautiful, dark brown hair, which hung half way down her back; her daughter's pride and joy. Her long hair was comparatively beautiful just like her sister's, Amy who had helped her so many times in caring for it.

Long hair that Dianna questioned the nurse about, as to how much of it would have to be removed for her daughter's shunt surgery. The nurse on the children's floor reassured mom as she was prepping the patient. Her response to the question that probably and most likely only a small area would be shaved on her head.

Dianna remembered how the nurse allowed Amy to climb into the bed next to her younger sister. So the two sisters could ride down the halls together toward the surgical unit as dad and mom walked along the side of their daughter's bed. Amy's presence there in the bed beside her sister, had a very calming effect on Angela. She just giggled all the way down the corridors, while she only looked at Amy, signing "Happy, love Amy."

The parents were so proud of fourteen-year old Amy that morning looking so strong and brave, not giving into tears in front of her sister. For earlier that morning the older daughter had confided in her parents how fearful she was for Angela's well being. Dad and mom tried to console their oldest by telling her to look upon the shunt emplacement as a positive, necessity toward her sister's health and that in a short time, Angela would be feeling so much better for her sake.

Just outside the pre-op room, Amy kissed and signed, "Love you," to her sister and than joined her Aunt Deb, Nana, Papa, Aunt Bet, grandparents and grandpa's sister Great Aunt Pauline, who were already in the surgical waiting room.

Frank and Dianna continued on into the pre-op room with Angela and the orderlies. Taking one glance around her, the now frightened girl saw and immediately knew where she was and started to react violently. The parents were asked to stay and help to hold their daughter down, along with three others on both sides of the bed; plus two male orderlies at her feet. All together it took ten people to restrain the very terrified and frightened patient in order for the nurse to give the injections. They could not believe the strength that she exerted in her attempts at kicking and biting to fight everyone off.

For the next few minutes as the pre-op injections started slowly taking affect, everyone stood there by her bedside. Her father feeling so helpless but at the same time he used his strength to hold down his daughter. Frank stood near the head of the bed, stroking her forehead while the mother stood close by holding her daughter's hand. Then Dianna was asked to gown up, so she could accompany her daughter into the operating room. They wanted mom to stay with her until their patient was completely under the anesthetic. Dianna remembered how she stood there next to the bedside staring down on Angela's face, with tears spilling, stroking her little girl's forehead and whispering to her deaf daughter, "Mom's here, I am so sorry that I helped them. I love you."

Dianna does not recall how long the surgery took, or what the family and everyone talked about as they all waited in the room. But it seemed and felt like forever before Frank alone was first to be summoned into the recovery area. The nurse replied she would come back and get mom in a little while. They wanted someone familiar there in the room next to the patient, as she would regain consciousness from surgery.

When it was Dianna's turn to go into the recovery room, one of the nurses stopped mom at the double door. She tried carefully to choose words to warn the patient's mother about what she would see regarding her daughter's appearance. The nurse also inquired if mom thought she would be able to handle the situation.

And this is what Dianna does recall as the double doors to the recovery room swung open. Anxious and very nervous she walked in and looked around, seeing so much activity, hearing numerous voices, and finally the wife saw her husband standing over in the direction on the left side of the large recovery area. Than Dianna saw Angela.

She was half sitting up against the partially raised bed. No hair! Completely bald! Dianna remembered how shocking and suddenly she halted dead in her tracks, precisely at that particular moment she felt faint. Mom was aware of activity all around within the room but her eyes were fixed on the daughter's head completely bald from no hair! As mother stared at her, Dianna remembered that she told herself, "Don't do it, Di," as she fought back the oncoming flow of tears "Don't faint! Smile and walk calmly over to your daughter. Angela needs her mother now."

She approached the bed and stopped. That's when Dianna saw a large surgical dressing on Angela's head and another one on the side of the neck.

Dianna glanced over at Frank. To her this man who seemed at that very moment so fragile but yet so strong. Don't remember if the young couple exchanged any words. For what was there to say? About two human beings who loved each other so much had felt the feelings together shared in their heart and had exchanged with their eyes. Silently together as one the two held hands and stood by their daughter's bedside, watching her slowly come out of the anesthetic.

As the young patient started coming around more, one of the many nurses came over to check on her. Angela stirred and struggled all the more insisting to sit up right. That's when she reached up and touched her head, discovering there was no hair! Whining pathetically, she fidgeted with and tore at the dressings, revealing the staple closures in her neck. When she started pulling at the IV in her hand, the nurse immediately restrained both arms to the bed railings.

Dianna remembered and will never forget Angela in her restrained position, looking up at Frank and at her mother. With wide, wild accusing eyes, as if to say, "You helped them do this to me!"

Mom had to turn away, to keep from crying. She does not remember what happened next. Those painful moments are locked away forever deep within her soul.

The next thing Dianna remembered was Angela being transferred to the Intensive Care Unit, via wheelchair. Normally patients who have been through major surgery are transferred out of recovery on a gurney or in their hospital bed. But that young patient insisted on getting out of that bed, led the doctor to allow her to sit up in a wheelchair. All the way back up to the pediatric floor and ICU, she ignored both her mother and father. A still picture, a quiet aura, very unusual calmness as she sat in the wheelchair. No fussing, no whining, just complete and total silence.

When the small group reached the Intensive Care Unit, Angela's bed wasn't quite ready, so they wheeled her over to a window. She sat there just staring out of it, with a blank expression on her face. Dianna placed a chair and sat down next to her daughter. Mom wanted and tried to get her little girl's attention, so she signed, "Nurse, fix bed, mom love you." But Angela would not look her way.

Frank decided it was time to leave and check on his other daughter Amy. While he was gone for the next several minutes, mother tried a couple more times though unsuccessfully to get her daughter to respond and to look over. Angela just shrugged her mother off. Mom knew she was feeling the hurt and embarrassment for the loss of her long hair. It made mother feel quite guilty and she knew that Angela was blaming her mother. But how could she understand? Mom had no explanation why they shaved her entire head! There was no simple way to explain.

Dianna hurt so badly for Angela. Her lovely veil seemed like the last of what was left of her daughter's dignity and pride, and even that was completely stripped away, back down the lower floors of the operating room. Mother knew Angela's hair would grow back and she desperately wanted to tell her daughter so. But right at that moment in time on that day, Angela would not allow herself to look, vocal or sign to her mother. So mom just sat next to her still beautiful little girl, quietly staring out the window and really not seeing anything.

Than Dianna remembered Frank coming back into the Intensive Care Unit and asking one of the nurses there if Angela's sister could come in for just a few minutes. The question she inquired how old Amy was? Even though Amy was under age, the nurse took compassion and consented when Frank explained how anxious the other daughter had been about her sister and how close the two girls were.

But first Frank stepped out into the hallway again to prepare Amy on how Angela's appearance. She started to choke up when dad told her how in surgery they completely shaved her sister's head. He also told her not to get upset if Angela ignored her, for she was probably confused and feeling embarrass without any hair, especially in front of her big sister.

Dianna will always remember that day and at that moment how proud she was of Amy. How she walked into the Intensive Care Unit. For she exhibited such strength of character when she first saw her younger sister, never reflecting in her face or attitude, how she was really feeling. Just being Amy and being there for Angela.

Angela stayed in the Intensive Care Unit for several days. And during the whole time she refused to have anything to do with her mother or her father; not even to look at them, avoiding eye contact, no signing and completely ignoring her parents. She was also very quiet and subdued. A new phase of her life that neither, mom or dad had never experienced before. Angela would respond to the nurses though, who were very good to her, in a very friendly, cooperative manner. Yet, another side of their daughter they never saw in the past when it had anything to do with a hospital.

Frank and Dianna told each other that they had to give her time; time to stop blaming them, time to accept and to be healed. But it still hurt and the guilt and blame on the parents' part never went away.

As usual during like any other hospital stay for Angela, the family was supported by family, close friends and her teachers through their prayers and hospital visits. One of Angela's teachers brought her a couple of brightly colored scarves to wear on her head. Even Dianna's sister, Sandi, who is confined to a wheelchair came up on her own, by using the local specialized transportation system. Dianna was so shocked and surprised to see her sister all alone waiting outside the Intensive Care Unit door.

Several days later, the patient was transferred out of the Intensive Care Unit and into the pediatric area, where she was given a private room directly across from the nurses' station. The location of her room allowed the nurses to observe their patient more closely. During this time Angela gradually came around responding to all of her family again.

The day of discharge, the neurologist was going to remove the staples. He got as far as removing two of the claps, when Angela started getting agitated and very upset and began pushing him away. So the doctor asked the father if he would do it, since she would probably trust her daddy more. Frank agreed and was instructed on how to remove the staples, using the tweezers-like instrument. The doctor's idea worked! Angela calmly sat there upon the bed, allowing her dad to remove the staples from her head, neck and belly.

Once at home though, Angela became reclusive and was very embarrassed if anyone outside of the immediate family saw her. She wouldn't even venture outside of the house for fear of someone seeing her. The spring days were nice and the family tried to coax her outdoors onto the deck to get some fresh air and sun.

Finally, one sunny day, wearing one of her scarves she agreed to go out in the back yard and have a picnic lunch along with Amy and mom. When the three of them had finished eaten, Dianna brought out some coloring books and crayons. There in the shade under a tree, Angela sat on a blanket quietly with her back toward the street side of the yard and was quite content for some time just coloring.

But, then some children came walking by and when they spotted the little girl with a scarf around her head, they stopped to stare, whispering among themselves as they pointed right at her. Mother ignored them hoping they would just go on their way of whatever. But their curiosity gave way to boldness (ignorance) and they shouted to Dianna over the fencing, asking what happened to her and why she didn't have any hair.

Even though Angela couldn't hear them, she sensed their inquisitiveness. Knowing it was about her she lowered her head as if trying to hide it from the children. Dianna answered them hoping to satisfy their curiosity so they would leave. But the children wouldn't stop staring and pointing even after mom tried and asked them to go. So Angela got herself up off the blanket and walked into the house to stay for the rest of the day.

And for the next three months, Angela would not leave the house. By September her hair had grown out into a short, pixie style that she even seemed to like and was comfortable enough around other people. Sporting her new hair do, which was cute and complimentary on her, the parents had their daughter's picture taken at a local department store. Amy did her sister's hair, makeup and chose an outfit for Angela to wear. This 20 x 14 portrait hangs on the wall in the parents' home and whenever Angela sees it, she signs "Me, Pretty," and giggles and giggles.

THE DECISION

Throughout all of Angela's young years, she had been through so much, unfairly too much for any one person to contend with in life. Thank God for the support, concern, love and prayers from family and friends. How many times was the family quoted that old adage? "God never gives you more than what you can handle." So true, the parents have learned. Dianna have found and still finds herself always wondering and asking, "Just how much more, God?" But during those hard times always thanking Him for seeing all of them through another crisis.

Most of all, Dianna thanked God for Frank, Amy and Angela for their strength and love that has always helped her through all the hard times the family had faced together. In turn, the parents thanked God for giving them two wonderful daughters, for those girls have been their bonding factor. Because of Angela and Amy, the husband and wife had accepted and love both of their daughters very much.

The oldest one being so mature early on, giving, loving, protective and so accepting of her younger sister. The youngest daughter for the special person she has been in their life, given Frank and Dianna a deeper value of love and a stronger commitment within their marriage. And thus, with and through everything transpiring in the family, their life's situation created a whole and stronger family unit based on love and sharing.

From Angela's very first hospital admittance after birth, right up to the last admittance for the shunt implant, so much has happened. So much has been dealt with through all the years of uncertainty if she would ever survive those first few days and months of seizures, pneumonia and other life threatening problems. The family had to learn, accept and deal with; living each day too its fullest and appreciating all the times, good and bad, they have had together.

How quickly time has passed and Frank and Dianna's daughters are becoming young women. Yes, the parents missed a lot with their girls and sacrificed a lot. But is that not part of life? Life is not a smooth road to travel, for anyone and we all have our own route to follow with its bends, turns and detours. And now they have come to another path in their family's journey together.

For Amy, her path in life will be that of college, a career, marriage and her own family some day. But what kind of path will there be for Angela?

For there was a huge, serious and frightening question that the parents knew some day had to be reckoned with sooner or later.

They came upon Angela's path much sooner than mom and dad ever anticipated. For all of them involved it was a heart-breaking but necessary decision, as to the life path that Frank and Dianna would have the final decision on. But all too soon after Angela's convalesce from the shunt surgery, her severe behavior and abusiveness returned in such an intense, agitated degree, that it was no longer possible for the family especially mother to care for her younger daughter in the capacity that was needed and required.

The family unit was once again being attacked, pulled and broken apart from Angela's problems. As the already exhausted parents (mentally and physically) once again were being drawn into the vortex of destruction, denial and guilt. Again, Dianna was on the verge of a mental break down and physical disability. She was facing a third back surgery and her mobility was severely impaired because of the lower back problems, making it impossible for her to physically handle her youngest.

And as before, Frank was burying himself in his work to avoid the mental stress and anguish that was going on in his home. He was fearful of his wife and daughter safety especially when his youngest daughter was in one of her numerous and frequent fits of rage, she had the resiliency of such physical strength that she could do bodily harm including to herself. Frank was silently enduring his own personal guilt and hell, and at the same time wanting to approach his wife to discuss other alternatives, but was afraid of her reactions and that she would reject him out of anger and hurt.

Amy did what she could and much more than what she should of to help her mother at home with her sister. And yes, Dianna's mother, mother-in-law, sister and sister-in-law helped out as much as they possibly could. They advised and urged Frank and Dianna to seek help, knowing they had to reach that final decision on their own and prayed that it would not be too late.

What was it that kept Dianna hanging on day after day, resisting the truth? The truth being she just couldn't care for Angela anymore. Was it guilt? Yes! It was guilt, but love guilt. A very young mother who had experienced the pain of childbirth, but found the joy and love for her infant. It was not the baby's fault that she came into the world with so many health problems. She didn't ask for her life the way it was. Her mother is the one who should be caring for her! The present and the future of one's life, their own well being while living on earth. Mom's retribution for her daughter's life suffering.

Was it fear? Yes. The worst kind of fear a person must face. The fear of what will happen to my child? Fear of Frank looking upon his wife as a failure, not only with her inability to care for his youngest one, but the fear and regret of having a defected daughter, and the hurt of knowing that the two of them would never have another chance for more children. Dianna always felt bad for not being able to try a third time for a boy, to carry on Frank's family name.

Those feelings of guilt and remorse, love and hurt, fed and haunted Dianna all at the same time. And that's what kept her going. It took Dianna until the summer of 1987 to come to terms with the cruel facts, and realize that she could no longer go on that way.

***

It all came to term on one particular day when Dianna's mother and father showed up unexpectedly. Hearing some commotion with Duke the beagle, barking in the yard, Dianna looked out the door to discover her parents coming through the back gate. Dad pushing the lawn mower before him and mom carrying the weed-whacker in one hand and the bright orange extension cord slung over her shoulder.

Dianna was so surprised and shocked to see them. She asked them, "What they were up to?" They informed their daughter that they had come over to do the yard because Frank's long hours at work and Dianna's physical inability and constant vigil with Angela, they had fallen behind in keeping the grass cut and trim. No problem! "The Yard Busters" had arrived!

Such an enduring moment, it brought tears to the young woman's eyes. To Dianna, her parents were so adorably cute and such a comical sight, dressed alike in blue jeans, matching sweatshirts, baseball caps and white tennis shoes. For such for a brief moment that day, her problems were forgotten, as she stood there looking at them, thinking how blessed and thankful to have them for her parents. Their presence made their daughter feel much better and later she would know exactly why?

Later that afternoon when the three of them had finished in the yard, Dianna confided in her mother about the grandmother's granddaughter.

She was going to tell Frank that his wife could no longer care for their daughter.

The daughter broke down sobbing. Mother and father hugged and consoled their daughter, by telling her what she was about to do was going to be the best thing for everyone concerned. They offered to stay with their granddaughters, so their daughter and husband could go away somewhere and talk in private with no distractions. So that very evening, Dianna and Frank drove out to a nearby Metro Park where they talked and opened up to each other, venting their feelings that had been suppressed for so many years.

***

In the tranquil surroundings of the park, the woman and the man sat on a wooden bench, near a pond and made their final decision. That particular late afternoon the park seemed virtually uninhabited around them. Although in the distance the woman could hear voices. Ducks glided silently through the still waters of the pond, birds chirped and sang, calling out to one another, and through this peaceful serenity the sun's raise came through the trees, casting a dream-like mesmeric atmosphere all around the couple.

The wife felt as if a great weight had been lifted from her soul and the calm surroundings was as if God, Himself, was shining down His benevolence upon His children in accordance.

Taking a deep breath, Dianna placed her hand within her husband's hand, as he sat there staring out over the pond. The only sound she was aware of at that moment was the beating of her heart, pounding deep within. Waiting patiently for his response, Dianna was reminded of a time, (was it only twelve years ago?) when a very young couple was pondering over another important decision.

EPILOGUE

The decision that the young couple had made that day as they sat hand in hand, looking out over the pond, surrounded within a beautiful and peaceful atmosphere of nature. A decision was contrived together, the most difficult, heartbreaking, frightening, but a necessary reality check of a life situation that neither one could or wanted to admit to the other.

That the two of them could no longer raise, help, give or live with their daughter, who desperately needed more from her parents then they could deliver. This act of passing the judgment on their daughter was finally reached with equal togetherness, acceptance, prayed over and felt so deep in the very core of oneself. A feeling that it was time, to accept and do the right thing.

To help their youngest daughter by admitting that outside help was needed immediately. To finally say, "I can't do it any longer, I'm too tired and frustrated. I must stop my running away from it. I need to give in. We must seek, reach out and look for help in the form of outside assistance."

***

This decision that my husband and I made together was extremely hard for both of us. We had finally decided that Angela needed aid, the kind that would come from others, professionals in the field of contributing and working with those with mental and physical disabilities.

I was told years back, when Angela was an infant that someday, I would have to seek other means, succor or perhaps give her to someone or something that could provide the necessary way of life for my little girl. It wasn't very easy back then to be told that by her doctor, who saw and knew what the future had in store for that child.

I on the other hand was her mother, determine to accept, deal and live with all problems of her disabilities. But that was only a mother's dream to be able to care for the child she brought into the world. Angela, my beautiful baby girl, my responsibility to care, provide, to give of oneself and most of all with love. But with all the love one can muster up, sometimes the love is not enough for a challenging, mental and physical disable child, who had also been diagnosed of having autistic tendencies. To watch the behaviors take over her life and see that she was really slipping further away from us each and every day.

So was it really fared to my daughter that her father and I said, "It's time." To make such an important decision about one's young life that would affect her as well as the rest of the family. In my mind yes because I knew mentally and physically, I just could not give her the proper care that she had to have in her life. Was it a selfish act on my part? At the time I was only thinking that there had to be another way to deal with her problems.

For I had come to a complete halt in my life and knew that I couldn't do it any longer. I could not take care of my little girl alone anymore. It was the truth. But the truth had made a difference in Angela's life and in her family's life as well.

Once the truth came out between Frank and I, the next important step but not an easy one was to tell our daughter Amy. She had to be told that her parents had come to a decision that her sister needed a special kind of help. This intervention would be very special, of what kind was unsure at the time and as the parents, we were not positive how, or where, when or what it would all involve.

For Amy had many questions and concerns about her sister that was already forming at the time within her own self. She wanted answers but mom and dad had none to give her at the moment. Frank and I told Amy it could be a possibility that Angela's care and help would come from outside the home. In other words Angela may have to leave our home in order to get the proper care and help.

This did not go over very well for our oldest daughter. She cried, became angry and upset at us first, for making such a decision in regards to her sister's life. Amy was young herself, how could she try and understand? Why would her parents give up on Angela? Why would her parents want to remove Angela from their home? What was wrong? Didn't mom and dad love her anymore? Of course down deep Amy knew in her heart that mom and dad loved Angela just as much as they loved her! Why? Why would they suggest for Angela to leave home? She knew her sister had many problems but the unknown answers were very frightening to a young girl who was extremely protective, caring and loving to her only sibling. Amy herself was growing into being a young woman.

Every new stage in life has difficulties, changes and experiences that one must learn to deal in order to live life. Amy had all those and now her sister's too. Yes, this was hard on our daughter and she wanted answers.

Some of the answers came when I contacted Angela's doctor, her school and her case manager from the Board of Mental Retardation. There were many arranged meetings that Frank and I had to attend in order to get the ball rolling.

Once I had made up my mind, accepted the decision, made that first phone call and asked for help, I knew that I couldn't turn my back on my daughter. Mom had to find a way, an answer and give her the proper help that she desperately needed as well as for the family.

This was not an easy task for me. It was very hard. Took many months, time, patience, phone calls, meetings and the support from my family. I asked my employer if I could take some time off from work. I explained everything, what I had to do for my daughter, my family, for myself.

I told them that my job was beginning to suffer. I just couldn't function as a good pre-school teacher 's aid and perform the duties until I functioned as a mother first. I always had felt I was good at my job with the children. But I could not give my best to other parents' children. Not until I could become useful to my own daughters at home.

Luckily my employer and boss were very understanding and allowed me to take time off from work. They were concerned first about my mental condition, my worries about Angela's problems, deep concerns about my other daughter and of course my relationship with my husband. They could see and knew that this situation was taking a terrible and horrible toll on their employee and her entire family.

With that they gave me not only the summer off but also an extended leave to take care of the situation at home. I have always appreciated their understanding, kindness and thoughtfulness that had been given to me.

✳✳✳

Another time when I thought and felt only loneness, despair, hopelessness and a feeling of darkness when someone else was kind and understanding about the family's situation. He ran a facility for severely mental, physical, and behavioral adults.

Frank and I went for an appointment one time to meet with him there. We first talked a great deal about everything happening to Angela, her mental and physical disabilities. Frank and I discussed how her behaviors and her self-abusiveness were taking over her life. As parents we felt at a lost as what to do for her and for our other daughter who was suffering too.

We completely and honestly, opened and bared our souls to a total stranger about our pain and stress. Frank and I opened the door to our inabilities and insecurities. He saw the pain that was written on our faces and he heard the fear from our mouths. This man sat patiently and waited until we were empty from within.

He gave us time, some suggestions, advice, information and a tour around his facility. At the end of our appointment he gave no reassuring answers to our problems. But he was understanding and kind to be honest enough to inform that this was definitely not the proper place to receive help for our young daughter. In fact the facility would be more harmful to her than any good.

Although we left that day feeling the same but at least he listened, cared and tried to give us some helpful information. At the end though he did make a comment that I still remember till this day and hold dear to my heart. He said, "Someday there will be light and you will find it at the end of the dark tunnel."

***

It wasn't until many weeks later that we received a phone call from Angela's case manager. She informed me that there was a small facility or group home in Cleveland. She suggested that Frank and I should go and see the place and talk to the people who ran and worked there.

At first my husband and I were somewhat hesitant and a little afraid to act upon her request. But after much discussion, I called and told the caseworker that we were interested. I gave her the go ahead to set the appointment with the day and time. Of course this meant that Frank had to get permission to be allowed to take time off from his job. But when the appointed day had arrived my husband and I felt nervous and scare about this trip to Cleveland with Angela's case manager.

Frank and I felt uneasy during the drive to the special facility. We both were feeling nervous, unsure, questioning and wondering if this was the right thing to do for our daughter. I think we both shared the same heavy blanket of guilt upon our shoulders that day. We had taken our next step. And it was a very hard, painful and difficult one to take as parents.

Our daughters meant so much to Frank and I. The four of us were supposed to be a family, living, working, playing, perhaps have a pet, go on vacations, share dreams and do it all together and with love. But our family life was different. Oh we worked, tried to play, had several pets that bothered and agitated Angela, there were no vacations, dreams of uncertainties but we did it all together with love. And with this love would come answers, help, a deeper spiritual growth that would someday down the road help heal the family's hurt and pain.

For each had to learn how to handle the life's disappointments and the cards that was dealt to our life style. Especially that very first year after the decision was made. Each one of us had to deal with it his or her own personal way. In fact Frank said, "It was a grieving period for all of us. But I felt like we were abandoning Angela."

When the three occupants in the car finally pulled up in front of an old, white complex building, the only one that talked first was Angela's case manager. We slowly approached the steps leading to the front entrance. Once reaching the front door Frank and I stood somewhat back and waited for someone to come and answer the bell.

The door was opened and a woman appeared behind the glass entrance. We stepped inside and immediately introductions were made to get the procedure started. She took us on a tour throughout the entire home, explaining all the uses of each room, answering questions or any concerns regarding the facility and staff. The director also asked some questions about our daughter as well.

We finally congregated in a room that looked like a living room area. Here we were told exactly how many clients they were able and allowed to take in on a permanent basis. At that particular time there were no openings and have course a waiting list of others. With that we felt that our interview was over and we thanked the director for her time.

Once more I felt defeated in trying to do the right thing for my daughter. On the way home Frank and I were somewhat quiet in the car, while Angela's case manager talked about the problem with most facilities was the waiting lists of so many families needing help. Also too there were not enough places for placements especially for a young person and up to the year of eighteen.

I felt that the day was a loss cause, unnecessary time taken from a job, frustrated and the constant questioning with myself if I was really capable of helping my daughter, whether it was at home or looking and finding some help in other areas.

For the next weeks ahead, I would continually hear, "We can't serve or help your daughter, there are no placements available or I can give you another number to call." The days ahead seemed long, hard, unbearable, emotionally and physically draining, and the outlook on Angela's and the family was bleak and dark for my search or quest to find help for my daughter and for the rest of the family.

There were other appointments made, time off from work, more meetings with questions and answers about certain group homes or facilities. It was very important to Frank and I to search for any possible help, explore all options, travel to different group homes and facilities. Although all the time, effort and energy seemed to begin with the same routine and ending with the outcome that brought us with the feelings of anxiety, fear, frustration and helplessness.

This was a battle of mixed emotions whirling within both parents. But as Angela's mother, I was determined to keep the faith, strength, and will power, my courage and win the war against the odds to find that bright light of hope.

Than one unexpected phone call came from Angela's caseworker informing me that a possibility of two doctors could give care and maybe the necessary help for Angela. It was that phone call to begin new changes in my daughter's life, her next five years.

To see and be part of good things that would occur, take place or happen within Angela's placement. But also to be involved and part of the unexpected, sad, hard, memorable and the unwanted memorable times or moments that took hold of her life and the family's as well. There would be tears of joy or sadness, giggles from laughter and love or the sounds of frustration and sadness that would shape her life into a young adult.

Not only for Angela but her family too would experience and share. Together all of us would grow mentally, physically and spiritually in the next five years, while Angela lived being cared and helped in a fostered or group home ran by the two doctors of physiology.

***

A day of hopelessness felt, when a family's destination to a group home, rode in silence except for the sounds of nervous giggles coming from Angela, who sat in the back seat. For each of them had to accept and face the future over a decision that the mother had brought to the husband's attention. The hurt and pain that touched the faces of the man and the eldest daughter, the other with fleeting moments being perplexed and agitated.

The short time spent helping with the unpacking and placing things in her new surrounding life. All the while trying desperately to keep the pain within, not allowing the sorrow to surface to bring about tears.

Parents and oldest sibling communicating by signing that the house and her bedroom were nice, new friends to help when she was angry; and most of all, "mom, dad and sister love you." The last signed words given to Angela, as her family silently left, leaving the distraught, frightened daughter and sister to her new surroundings and circumstances.

The family was met with so many challenges starting with a month of no physical connection. Director's felt this was necessary for Angela's adjustment period. Daily phone calls to check on her progress to still feel connected. Just hearing about her days was so extremely hard on the family but much harder on their daughter.

The worst day was on Thanksgiving. The parents, one daughter, grandparents, aunt and uncle with their two sons sat around the table. They gave thanks to God and asked for blessings upon the family, the meal and for the special one not there. Each one had to deal with his or her turbulent emotion. A day of thanks, a day of sadness, a day of shared love and a day that left its mark.

But this way of life only lasted until her age of seventeen. During the five years there were many stress factors such as issues of money, threatening conversations to discontinue her placement, questions with her safety and well fare all lend to many meetings, phone calls and even letters to the State Represenitive for help in order to keep what I had worked so hard for my daughter.

I was afraid that she would lose her waiver, her social security benefits and her place within the system, I had worked too long and hard; and I wasn't about to lose everything for her without a fight. This meant even a fight with those who in the beginning had the right desire and intention in helping others. An unexpected and extremely intense contraversary with words, action and a strong conviction that I wasn't going to give up without a result leading to the best solution for my daughter's best interest at heart.

What really happen from this intense situation led to many meetings once again with Angela's case managers and new providers who represented another facility willing to take, help and care for our daughter. They introduced to us the idea of placing our daughter in the community, living in an apartment or rented housing, sharing with another adult with the same disabilities, (housemate) and having twenty four hour staff at all times.

We talked about transportation to and from school and what school would be good for Angela. Everyone new that she did not mainstream very well in high school surroundings. For that experienced was a complete disaster! Also the directors pointed out the responsibilities about the care of Angela, addressing her medical issues, doctors, goals and expectations, staff learning sign language in order to communicate with their client, finances, safety issues involving the home and traveling time, activities within the home and also outside in the community.

Another essential point for discussion was who would be living and sharing the home environment with our daughter? Frank and I wanted and insisted upon a female to be living with our daughter. After some time, search and attention to another couple that had a daughter also that could be serve in the community by a provider.

A young woman around Angela's age was selected and once again another meeting was held to meet the parents, discuss and decide about what kind of housing, number of staff on duty during the twenty-four hour period, date and time of moving the girls into their new housing, getting them together several times before the actual move and other duties or obligations for the program.

My husband and I met on several occasions with the other girl's parents, looked into several different apartments around certain areas that we all felt would be a safe environment for our girls.

Than Frank and I were informed that the other parent knew someone who had a duplex for rent. So everyone met again to see the building, the grounds (apple orchard), meet the landlord, discuss the monthly rent, talked about the girls living in the lower level (two bedrooms), move in date and what kind of items the girls would need to furnish their home.

We also planned and had a house warming party for our daughter and invited family and friends. Another very important issue was informing the landlord about the girls (renters), they're disabilities and who would be caring for them (staff) day and night. Both young women were deaf; both knew signing, both had other medical problems and both girls had behavioral problems from time to time. But each young lady had her own particular way of showing her frustrations, behavior outbursts or abuse to herself or perhaps to others. This was very important that the landlord had to know and understand because he would be renting out his duplex to young women with disabilities.

When the big day arrived for Angela to move into her new place to live, I think not only Angela felt unsure, insecure and questioned the new placement, but Frank and I also felt some apprehension. For this was a very big step and move in our daughter's life. None of us had any experiences about this new lifestyle that Angela would be involved with the placement, new providers, staff and now a housemate.

I had made several phone calls to other parents about their special child living in this new community way of life. They all spoke very highly of the program and how well their son or daughter were doing. After hearing from other parents, I did feel somewhat better about my daughter's new adventure into life. Besides Frank always wanted Angela to live a normal life as possible.

This Community Living Option would open the door for Angela, giving her a life that we all sometimes take for granted. Along with the staff, performing activities within the community, she would go shopping, choose her clothing, buy groceries, do certain chores, cook and bake, do laundry and learn how to care for her home. This would be Angela's new placement, a very special way of life, but a dream finally coming real for our daughter.

For the next five years our daughter experienced a kind of life that Frank and I thought would never happen for her. Our decision-making back then brought constant changes in her life. Even though we gave Angela over to people that could do more for her, we as parents have always been involved with all decisions regarding our daughter.

Through the help from an attorney who has shown so much care, concern, effort in time and legal help and advice through the years, helped me to obtain legal guardianship in behalf of my daughter.

Even though Angela lives outside our home, we are still very much a family. We visit her at her place, bring her home for visits, she's always part of family functions, we are still a family. But our family has extended to those who have a real special uniqueness about them in caring for those who have and live with disabilities.

The provider sent out a news magazine focusing on those people who receives the services. In the spring issue of 1995 there was a picture of our daughter Angela, attending her graduation prom with her sister Amy.

Prior to the dance, Amy had gone out with her mother and together found two identical outfits that Angela and Amy could wear to the event. At that time Angela had absolutely nothing to do with dresses! So big sis found a very cute answer to the "dress" issue. She found black and white small checker slacks, dressy and comfortable white tops and black dress slip on shoes. For her little sister a long black beaded necklace, small white beaded earrings and bringing the whole outfit together an adorable big black hat with a beautiful sunflower on it!

Mom had ordered a wrist corsage for Angela and Amy lovingly placed it on her sister's wrist. The picture shows the two sisters standing together under a flowering arch. It is truly a photograph that the parents are very proud to have two exceptionally beautiful, talented each in their own way, giving and loving daughters.

The written article "Angela in Supported Living" states that she received the Year award in recognition of her progress and accomplishments. It was written how she came into the program with a severe reputation and many challenging behavioral issues. Talked about her progress that year had been nothing short of remarkable, resulting from hard work by Angela, along with support from family and staff.

Mentioned how being consistent, communicating effectively through sign language and taught Angela to schedule and fulfill her responsibilities which the outcome made her happy. Angela was better able to perform tasks such as grocery shopping, cooking and attending school with a lower level of anxiety. The issue reported how wonderful to see such good changes and highly congratulated our daughter.

The following school year Amy again drove and attended her sister's prom. But this time Amy had lent her younger sister one of her own prom dresses, a powder blue mid length dress, in hopes that she would wear it. She did!

***

During those years, her age of being almost eighteen to twenty one, we watched Angela grow into a beautiful woman and saw the many accomplishments. She adjusted with some behaviors when new changes came about in her life. Changes such as staff turnover, two other new housemates, new housing placement (for the other fell through), schools and teachers, medical and health problems and a change within her own family.

Her sister Amy got engaged and married, in which Angela was very involved with the bridal shower and the wedding. The day of her sister's wedding, she walked down the aisle on her daddy's arm. So beautifully dressed in peach, an outfit Amy and I found for her to wear. Frank said, "Today I was proud and lucky to walk both of my lovely daughters down the aisle."

A very important day because Angela now had a brother-in-law, Don. He came into Angela's life giving her consideration and love. Sometime later another new arrival came into our family. For Angela was now called "Aunt Angie."

Right from the very beginning Angela showed so much love and affection toward her niece. Her motherly instincts came forth in a loving and caring way for the baby. She gave Kalyn her bottle, always watched and helped her sister in the actual care of the baby, she would sit and hold her and play with her niece in her own special way. As Kalyn grew so did the bond between aunt and niece.

Angela's sister, Amy has always been part of her sister's life. Amy is very dear and special to Angela. Not only a big sister always being around but now Angela also has Don and Kalyn as well. For they have become such a big part of her life. Amy remembers watching her sister holding Kalyn in her arms and giving the bottle.

As her niece grew and started to hold onto her own bottle, Angela while holding her would gently remove her hands away from it. For this was the aunt's job to hold the bottle for her niece. Also Angela enjoyed helping with her baths and dressing her niece. For that too became Angela's job!

And Kalyn's father, Don has learned how to be around Angela, shows respect, kindness, love and helps to celebrate the good times and moments in his sister-in-law's life. He also supports his wife when things go bad, rough, sad or hard for his wife's sister.

***

Well you know life wouldn't be life if there weren't ups and downs, times of trouble, hardships and disappointments. We do not live in a world with everything running smoothly. In life people have to make decisions, accept the outcome of them and then move on. That's exactly what Frank and I had done all the years with Angela.

The decision we made for our daughter with the new provider went well for almost five years. But Angela started to develop severe behavioral problems that affected her life, the staff, school, within the community and even being around with her family.

Perhaps because of her having autistic tendencies the changes with staff turnover, changes in housemates (once having a male), medical problems (voiding and going blind now in the left eye), changes in medications or just growing and developing into adulthood had brought out more uncontrollable behaviors.

Behaviors so severe that she was abusing herself and others around her, the staff for example were afraid of her and take downs or gentle restraining was becoming very difficult and numerous day and night. She would become so agitated and frustrated so easily and tear into her house by completely destroying her bedroom.

We would receive phone calls from the staff and inquiring if Frank, Amy and I could visit even more often, thinking that more visits and time spent with the family would help. But this did not help our daughter or solve anything and she was becoming more and more severe in her behaviors.

I remember getting a phone call one evening from a staff asking if we could come over to Angela's house, for she was having behaviors and really a bad night. So the three of us headed over and found her in the bedroom surrounded by a complete destruction of her room. She had pulled the dresser drawers out, a couple were broken, clothing everywhere and some were torn, she attacked the window and broke the glass, pulled the blinds down and tore the curtain from the rod, her bedroom was in a complete disarray. She even had punched holes in the walls.

We stayed late and help to put order back to her bedroom, comfort and consoled our daughter and talked, gave support to the staff and made sure that Angela would be alright before leaving for home. No one knew what was really happening to Angela, had no answers even after checking into all her medications, looked at her medical problems for results or answers, nothing seemed to help to control our daughter.

The situation was only getting worse and her behaviors were becoming so severe, intense and increasing, along with the constant restraining staff was now doing in controlling her during the behavior attacks. Finally the providers thought it was time for another meeting with the family.

The providers, case manager, some staff and Angela's family met to discuss what could be done, issues looked into on how we could provide the proper care for my daughter. We talked about the medical problems, medications, the concept and the importance use of gentle restraining, behaviors that caused abuse to self, the staff and what and how the family could also help and do.

One option was to have the director from the behavior program and their staff come out to Angela's home and worked with the facility's staff for retraining. They would spend time in the home, work with staff and Angela, get to really know our daughter and understand her needs. The family would also spend time with Angela in her home with the special behavioral staff by talking and giving whatever information they needed to know about our daughter.

Frank and I communicated and explained about her medical background. With Amy's devotion and love for her sister, she gave so much feedback to them about her sister's likes and also her dislikes. The accomplishments; and things we thought as a family she was capable of still doing, if only somehow and someway the behaviors could be controlled.

Amy was such a great daughter and sister during this emotional and stressful period in Angela's life. She found strength enough to get not only herself through this ordeal but she gave of herself to her sister, parents and others who wanted to help Angela.

The three of us was a team for Angela and we were determine to do whatever it took to pull our girl out from the hell she was living in. We were there working, helping, caring, loving, supporting, communicating in sign language. When Angela's regular housing staff was unable, unavailable or just taking some time away from the stressful situation.

***

Another time I remember was when Frank and I were called again to Angela's house late one evening. The director from the facility asked if we could stay with our daughter that evening, through the night and until around 8:00A. M., the following morning. They were short on staff and she mentioned that someone would definitely be there at our daughter's house the next morning.

Of course we had our own thoughts and feelings why? Word had got out about Angela's severe behavioral problems and the staff was beginning to feel uneasy, afraid and apprehensive about wanting to work in our daughter's home. Even those who worked on the base facility refused to work at her house because they heard such horror stories and a few were bit during her many horrible struggle the take-downs occurred.

In a way we couldn't blame the workers because as a family we witnessed Angela's anger, the severe behavior, self-abuse and the whirl wind destruction in her home.

So Frank and I arrived at Angela's front door with our small overnight bag. We walked in and saw no one in the living room but we did hear some noises in the front bedroom. Both of us looked at each other and started into the small hall that led into our daughter's bedroom. There we found Angela on the floor in the middle of the room, looking very agitated biting at her hands and amid the disarray of her clothing, bedding and dresser drawers.

She had a behavior right before we arrived, the staff informed her parents. Not for sure want brought it on or triggered it, just that she exploded so fast. Once again we tried to comfort our daughter who sat on the floor of her room still biting at her hands, arms and legs; and at times pounded herself on the chest while making sad, vocal noises.

Frank and I started to put the bedding back on her bed, drawers back in the dresser and other little things back in place or near it. The window was not touched because it had been covered with plywood that Frank had put up from the time before. After we had finished the staff had left for the night, and mom and dad were left alone with their daughter.

One of us signed to Angela that mom and dad was going to sleep at her house. A bed was made on the couch for our daughter and Frank and I put a blanket down on the living room floor where he and I slept during the night.

***

There is also another incident that happened with my daughter, an emotional and heart breaking moment that I can still envision to this very day. Late one night Angela was sitting on the sofa and I was on the floor in a kneeling position facing her. It was another very bad night at the house and Angela had one of her terrible behavior episode.

She was still somewhat agitated and biting at her hands. I tried to rub her hands and arms gently, while signing, "Please no bite hand, hurt you." I continue to show attention to her, carefully and gently touching and rubbing her hands. I looked up at the tortured face of my little girl and saw the unhappiness and pain etched across that tormented child.

That's when for the first time I saw my daughter crying, she actually had tears. Usually when Angela was upset she would display it by abusing herself or making a very sad and forelorning vocal sounds. But not only tears, she looked at me, her mother and signed, " help." I was shocked and surprise that she asked for help. Angela knew that something was happening to her and she was reaching out to her family.

I remember kneeling in front of her and signing back, " Mom will help you, I love you." That moment on I realized that if I didn't do something immediately, that my husband, Amy and I could possibly lose someone very special in our life.

That night after Frank and I made sure that everything was safe enough and under control with Angela and her caregiver, mom and dad left for home. At first we were quiet in the car, both Frank and I caught up in our own personal thoughts about what was taking place in our daughter's life.

I remember that my husband broke the silence between us first. He made a statement saying that we had to do something but he just didn't really know what at the time. He said that he felt helpless and hopeless and at a complete loss. Angela was getting worse with her behaviors, the self-abuse and destruction to the home. The caregivers were tired, at a loss, there were more take downs or restraining with Angela.

Frank and I were quite concern how long the providers were willing to care for our daughter. The many questions and concerns they had about their client, her safety and of others. What can we, the provider and family, do to make Angela's life better? How long can they actually give the proper care for her? What was really appropriate in care giving?

Perhaps another reality check, the question about looking into another facility in placement for our daughter. Again so many concerns, more unanswered questions, worries, fears and the horrible feeling that we could lose Angela if the right kind of help was not provided for her.

I sat quietly and emotionally drained in the front seat of our car that night. I stared straight ahead and listened to my husband 's saddened voice as he tried to talk. And at the same time playing over and over in my mind the scene, the image of my little girl sitting on the sofa whimpering from within, with tears and signing to me, her mother, "help."

With my hands laying on my lap, my eyes focusing on the car lights and tears in my eyes, I responded in a shaky voice, "Frank, I don't know, my shoulders feel so heavy with this burden, it's too great for me to handle alone. I am going to put this in God's hands, in His hands."

That night was a new beginning for me. I had placed Angela and all concerns, difficulties and problems into the Hands of One, Who would hear my constant prayer for help and guidance.

With much praying from all of us, the family once more was notified of another meeting to discuss Angela's progress if any. Unfortunately with everyone involved over at her house, she still had made no headway in her behaviors at home or in school. The next step was to talk about removing Angela from the house and placing my daughter on the facility base in a behavioral unit. She would be removed from the home setting and environment and put in a unit on the main facility or base with other severe behavioral clients.

After the meeting a tour was given to the family. But our daughter Amy had already knew what the behavioral unit looked like and everything consisted because she had worked in that unit. Even though Amy had knew the well trained specialists, she knew down deep in her heart that this was not the correct answer for her sister. The environment most likely would cause her sister to become worse and not better.

We as a family would lose Angela and her life would be lost. The facility had offer hope and a bright light at a very dark time, gave endlessly of themselves, worked hard with Angela and educated their employees for their client, cared twenty four hours and seven days a week and love throughout it all.

Amy knew her sister, all that she had been capable of and all that she could still be capable to do in life. This was not the correct environment setting and Amy told her mother and father. Our oldest daughter voiced her opinion for her parents to look elsewhere. Elsewhere Angela's family did and once again a new decision was made but one of "Bittersweet."

***

Because You Love Me
On April 21, 2002, my husband Frank and I had celebrated our wedding anniversary of thirty years. But it seemed like yesterday we were only

young adults of eighteen, saying to each other the sacred words of marriage. Words that is very meaningful between a man and woman with God as their witness declaring their undying love for each other.

In front of a priest, their family and friends, that young couple had exchange vows to promise to each other their love, devotion, staying true and honest throughout marriage, supporting each other in time of health and in sickness and never giving up especially when times of heartaches and troubles.

At that time those words were spoken with love and perhaps also along with a little fear. For this couple was only eighteen, not out of high school yet, but facing to be parents in four short months.

But because you, Frank, loved me, and continues to this day, our love for each other has made us one and we together share a beautiful and wonderful life. A life we can be proud of, that we shared with our two daughters, Amy and Angela.

For thirty-two years we lived and experienced love, happiness, times of troubles and sadness, along with so many illnesses. But a marriage and life that has given us so many rewards. Such rewards as these are gifts from God.

These gifts I speak of are family and friends. The rewards are results from working very hard in marriage, in life. On April 27, 2002, our daughters Amy and Angela gave us a surprise anniversary party at our home with the help of family and friends.

She called on everyone's attention to a song sung by Celine Dione that would be dedicated to Frank and I, from her sister Angela. With tears in her eyes, Amy said in a choked voice, "If my sister could speak right now to express her love, gratitude and thanks to dedicated parents, this song and these words would describe how she feels. The song I am speaking of is called, "Because You Love Me."

While the song played Frank and I listened carefully to the words as everyone else did. Throughout the song my eyes kept returning in the direction of my youngest, Angela. The song expresses love, giving of self and how love can change one's life. Here are some of the lines that describe Angela, how her parents and sister saw her through the twenty-seven years of her special life.

***

"For all the times you stood for me
For all the joy you brought to my life
Every dream you made come true
You were my strength when I was weak
You were my voice when I couldn't speak
You were my eyes when I couldn't see
You saw the best that was in me
You were my inspiration
My world is a better place because of you
I am everything I am, because you love me."

***

Twenty-nine years ago when I gave birth to my second daughter, I recalled how she was conceived with love. Through twenty-nine years my daughter knew from day one that she was loved.

It's because of that strong feeling, that emotion has brought and taken our daughter through all obstacles of life. This love has come in many forms, such as from her family and friends, doctors, nurses, teachers, specialists, caregivers from different agencies and the many other people that have encounter our daughter.

But especially from her big sister Amy, her dad and her mom. It's a kind of love that comes when one is faced with an incident in life that you cannot change; but you can try and work very hard, pray and keep faith and ask God for help and guidance to make a difference.

For the last eight years we have seen such a beautiful and wonderful change in a young woman's life. This transformation in one's young life was not caused by changes of appearances, or health problems miraculously taken away. She still remains to be the same daughter born with all her health issues.

She has the same big sister Amy, same mom and dad, brother-in-law Don and a niece Kalyn a nephew Kaleb. She still has her grandma and grandpa, her Nana, aunts and uncles along with their new additions. But in the last eight years she acquired a new family and friends who have given our daughter and sister a "Bittersweet Life."

I am speaking about a wonderful place in Whitehouse, Ohio, called Bittersweet Farms for the adults who have autism. The mission of Bittersweet, Inc. is to maximize opportunities for individual development of persons with autism by providing an array of premier services to individuals and support families.

Angela lives in her own home that was bought through her parents. She has a housemate, a woman who is also autistic. Back when Angela had signed to mom for help, a new decision was made, one of "Bittersweet." From out of darkness a bright light, a burden so heavy that was placed in God's hands, an answered prayer. Help was given to our daughter. But through all the dark and hopeless days, something good came from something so tragic. Our daughter Angela was able to help another person in life. These two women have bonded as housemates and become truly good friends, who care about each other.

Angela is truly living the life that her father, sister and I had always wanted for her. She lives in her own home with a friend, both being served twenty-four hours with care and love. Our daughter does all the things that we take for granted in life. She is taught and through daily supervision is helped to care for her home. With the caregivers help she enjoys choosing and preparing meals in the kitchen through her skill development program. Angela assist with housekeeping tasks and has choices of these tasks to do. The caregivers use pictures in helping her to select. Angela loves to do laundry and has the skills along with assistance from staff to sort clothes and set the correct buttons on the machines. She also works along side with staff performing some yard chores.

Also her friends, the caregivers supervise and assist with her personal care. Angela likes to make herself pretty and takes much pride in this aspect of her self. The caregivers help her to achieve this goal. She loves to use makeup, brushing and fixing her hair, having her finger and toenails painted; staff also has a girl day outing for hair and eyebrow waxing appointments.

She likes shopping for beauty items. Angela simply has fun shopping with the caregivers or with her family. She shops twice a week. With assistance she selects and chooses items for groceries and for her personal things. Other community outings with the caregivers are eating out, movies, parks, zoo trips, rolling skating and camping. Angela loves to go to Cedar Point, in Sandusky, Ohio and ride all the rides, roller coasters and all! Angela also enjoys visiting the homes of the caregivers and meeting their families as well.

Angela is a collector of pictures and carries these photographs with her all the time. She has many pictures of her family and her "Bittersweet" friends. The caregivers know and realize how important the family means to their client. There are times when family will receive letters and pictures written or drawn by Angela with the help from the staff.

During the week, Monday through Friday, she works on the eighty acres of the farm at Bittersweet. There are set chores or goals in horticulture, wood making, the barn in caring for the variety of animals, gardening, weaving or perhaps chores in the main house in the kitchen or laundry area.

Angela and her friends, the other clients who live on the farm also create and make many items that are sold during their yearly Spring Flower Sale, Fall Harvest Festival and the winter Christmas trees and craft sale. When not working Angela likes hanging out with her friends, picnics, holidays and celebrating birthdays, swimming, riding her three-wheeler and hiking with her friends on Saturday mornings. Although she is known to be a slow hiker!

She really takes delight in working with fabrics with loom making and creating potholders, placemats, table runners, rag rugs, pillows and so many other craft items. Angela made a beautiful rag rug with decorative flowers and gave it to her parents for a cherished gift. She has made pillows and received red ribbon second place at the Fulton County Fair for her workmanship.

Along with a framed blue ribbon Achievement Award for pillow making that hangs proudly in her living room. These pillows were given to her parents and are very much appreciated and cherished. She made a loom material wind sock with a label attached, made by Angela which mother found and bought at the Fall Harvest Festival. Angela has tried her hand at wood making and was learning how to use different tools. She has learned how to saw wood by using the old fashion two man saw.

They learn how to work in the gardens because everything they grow is used on the farm for the many variety of uses for their crafts. They learn how to dry flowers for the many different craft items for making, creating and decorating. She enjoys working on three, four or more steps of projects. Angela enjoys showing off her work, making and giving crafts to family and friends that she herself have made on the farm.

Angela has worked in the barn caring for the horses and learned how to ride one of them. In fact we have pictures of our daughter riding on one of their horses (Bulwinkle, a retired police horse, but now is deceased) wearing the proper headgear and being led around by a worker holding a rope. The smile on her face is so rewarding because in the picture the accomplishment was visible.

Her family will always remember the day when she fed the horse just one straw at a time. She was in no hurry to feed and the horse was very patient waiting to be fed. Also they learn how to care for the other animals such as rabbits, chickens, ducks, goats and llamas. Sometimes they care for the pigs to fatten them up for the Harvest Fest.

All the staff or caregivers and clients have become her family our extended family. With the staff they have learned how to communicate with our daughter. They are all very caring, devoted, hardworking and loving to their clients. The caregivers and other staff management are pressed to focus on their yearly goals, skill developments, assisting with fire and other safety issues within home and in transportation.

Monitoring with independence with self-administration of breathing treatments, assistance with administration of medications, motoring for seizures and her asthma. They monitor her health, assist to schedule and attend medical, dental and eye appointments.

They work and follow a behavioral program and work on goals that are specified. Also they provide proper intervention for her outbursts or behaviors as needed. Staff, management, her caseworker and family meet throughout the year to discuss Angela's service plan.

With everyone working together and communicating, Bittersweet Farms have created an atmosphere of family, loving and nurturing, working and supporting, giving and helping those with autism to live a fulfilling and rewarding life.

Through all of her accomplishments and being so productive in life our daughter has confidence, feels good about her, is content, shows love and affection toward others. She is finally truly happy with the sounds of her giggles.

Even though she has another family to love and share her life with, Angela is still very much part of our family's life. She comes home on some weekends, holidays, all family functions, birthday parties and overnights at her sister's house to spend time with her niece and nephew that she enjoys playing and even caring and doing things for them.

Kalyn is eleven years old and along with her seven-year old brother Kaleb, there are many of their friends who are acquainted with Aunt Angie. When their aunt is spending time at their home, much attention and love is shown and given to Angela.

Just like when Amy was little and her friends had shown love, attention, played and even learned about someone different because of mental and physical disabilities. We are all unique, special and we all can learn and be challenge from each other as we go through life as God's family.

For God gave Frank, Amy and I a challenge in life, He gave Angela to live out that challenge. I believe so strongly in my heart that we as a family have accepted, lived and experienced, scarified and been rewarded, and each one of us has been blessed with our life at present.

As a family we will continue to travel on his or her road, living one day at a time, accepting and dealing whatever God and life will put before us.

We will continue to love and support one another as we journey into the future. I no longer dwell on the past or worry about what lies ahead, for God will be there, always listening and answering our prayers.

But I do so much enjoy my present life with my husband Frank, with Angela, her extended family, Amy and Don, and my grandchildren, Kalyn and Kaleb. And every day I thank God for them.

I thank Him also for all others who have been placed in our life, our families and friends who have stood by us throughout the years, giving to us their love and support. Angela and her family have been taught to be strong, keep faith, accept, deal and work with it and pick up our crosses and continue on in life. But most of all God has taught us how to really live life with giggles.

Today Angela has another wonderful and beautiful reason to giggle. On October third of 2003, she received an ocular prosthesis (artificial left eye). Now my little girl wants to smile for the camera and giggles with both of her eyes.

On February 16, 2005 Angela will be thirty years old. God has given a bright light at the end of once a very dark tunnel. This light shines forth for all with many giggles.

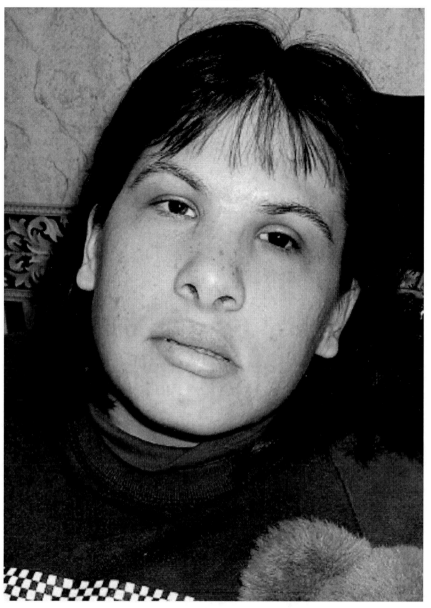